Discovering Stained Glass in Detroit

By NOLA HUSE TUTAG
with Lucy Hamilton

Photographs by Dirk Bakker   Drawings by Hope Palmer

WAYNE STATE UNIVERSITY PRESS   DETROIT   1987

Library of Congress Cataloging-in-Publication Data

Tutag, Nola Huse, 1922–
  Discovering stained glass in Detroit.

  (Great Lakes books)
  Bibliography: p.
  1. Glass painting and staining—Michigan—Detroit—
Catalogs. I. Hamilton, Lucy. II. Title. III. Series.
  NK5312.T88 1987 748.59174′34 87–16066
  ISBN 0-8143-1874-6 (alk. paper)
  ISBN 0-8143-1875-4 (pbk. : alk. paper)

This publication is supported by grants from the Michigan
Council for the Arts, the Humanities Department of the College
of Liberal Arts of Wayne State University, and the Stained Glass
Publication Fund.

Contents

Foreword

Stained glass is an extremely visible but sadly neglected aspect of our national heritage. Its glowing colors not only dramatically enrich interior spaces but provide a wealth of information about the religious philosophy, economic growth, and artistic taste of our country. The efforts by the Detroit community to study and publish its stained glass are a most impressive undertaking. Too frequently have architectural surveys presented the buildings in a city with almost no attention to the murals, wall tiles, stained glass, woodwork, or lighting of the structures. Yet, in many cases, especially with churches, it is primarily these decorative elements that reveal the social and religious identity of the buildings to their patrons.

Detroit is indeed fortunate that its public institutions and its religious congregations have preserved a wide selection of the art of stained glass. Excellent examples of medieval figural glass are on display in the Detroit Institute of Arts, and impressive heraldic panels can be seen in the Edsel & Eleanor Ford House. (All of these windows are to be included in *Stained Glass before 1700 in American Collections: The Central and Western States* [*Corpus Vitrearum Checklist III*]. The book is part of the National Gallery of Art's *Studies in the History of Art: Monograph Series I.*) "Modern" glass is in great abundance and of extraordinary variety in Detroit: the Munich School work of Mayer and Company, the opalescent windows of Louis Comfort Tiffany and John La Farge, the Gothic revival works of Charles J. Connick, and the modern expressions of Frank Lloyd Wright, among many others.

It is imperative to educate both the public and the scholarly community to the importance of glass. Unlike most other forms of art, which achieve security as "collectibles," able to be bought, sold, and exchanged, stained glass is a public art and therefore depends on the public responsibility for its appreciation and survival. This well-illustrated and broad survey of so many fine examples of Detroit's stained glass will help us to better understand the so-called lost art that is in reality all around us.

Virginia C. Raguin, Ph.D.
College of the Holy Cross
Worcester, Massachusetts
Director, Stained Glass Census in America

Acknowledgments

Discovering Stained Glass in Detroit owes its existence to many people who have given their enthusiastic support and encouragement. My first thank you goes to my husband, Edward J. Tutag, for his support and faith. Second, my deep appreciation goes to Lucy Hamilton who suggested this sabbatical topic to me several years ago, and who, in the last year of my work, has given her help in every possible way to nurture this guide into existence. Third, my thanks to Professor Homer Edwards of Wayne State University who for three summers accompanied me to study and photograph churches and buildings. His encyclopedic knowledge of churches and stained glass was my inspiration. Fourth, my sincere thanks to Professor Bernard Goldman, former director of the Wayne State University Press, my mentor, chief supporter, and good friend for encouraging and supporting this project from the beginning. Richard Kinney, former director of the Press, and Jean Owen, chief editor of the Press, have listened, encouraged, and prodded, and to them I give thanks. Special appreciation goes to Peter Barnet, assistant curator of European Sculpture and Decorative Arts, Detroit Institute of Arts, who enthusiastically supported and helped the project from the beginning and who wrote the comments and the major portion of the entries from his department. William Kessler, noted international architect, Dr. Virginia Raguin, director of the Census of Stained Glass in America, and Mark Talaba, stained glass artist, receive sincere appreciation for their invaluable help and contributions. Dirk Bakker and Hope Palmer have added immeasurably to the pleasure of producing this guide with their handsome and beautiful works of art. And special thanks to the artists Lucille and Jim Nawara for additional drawings. Gloria Parker, Marianne Letasi, and Adrienne Odom have my gratitude for their willingness to help and for their graciousness. A very special and indispensable person has been Louise Dezur, who has patiently translated my handwriting and my typewriting to the word processor. Anne Adamus, editor of the Wayne State University Press, and Lillian S. Sims have struggled with the manuscript, and the edited version is a joy to behold.

Others have helped in very significant ways and each one of the following must know how much I have appreciated their help and suggestions. Michael Young of London, England, who worked with Wendy Evans of the Museum of London and Robert Howell of the Victoria and Albert Museum to produce very valuable research material on the window in St. Peters Episcopal Church; the humanities staff of the Wayne State University College of Liberal Arts, especially professors Martin Herman and Marc Cogan for their total support; Professor Richard Bilatis, chair of the Art and Art History Department, Wayne State University, for his contribution to the book; from the Detroit Institute of Arts—Nancy Shaw, curator, Sarah Hufford, associate curator, and Jim Tottis of the American wing, Patience Young, associate curator of the Education Department, and especially Carla Reczak and Kyra Curtis of the library; James Bridenstine, director of the Edsel & Eleanor Ford House for the valuable information on heraldic shields; William Worden, director of the Historic Designation Advisory Board of the City of Detroit, for his help and especially for loaning valuable photographs of the ship *City of Detroit III;* Greg Wittkop, associate curator from the Cranbrook Academy of Art Museum for research material; Timothy Husband, associate curator Metropolitan Museum of Art, the Cloisters; Dr. Dorothy Kostuch, Center for Creative Studies, for her interpretation of the Cass Avenue Methodist window; Peter Blum, historian of the Stroh Brewery Company for the photograph and for his helpful research; Mr. and Mrs. Aid Kushner and Rabbi Hertz of Temple Beth El; Donna Swanson, artist, and Donald Sammick, president, of the Lamb Studios for their valuable research materials and photographs; Helene Weis, librarian of the Willet Studios for her interest, help, and photographs; Gabriel Mayer of Mayer Studios, Munich, Germany; Paul Ganz, media relations representative of Michigan Consolidated Gas Company; Elizabeth Yakel, Archivist for the Roman Catholic Archdiocese; to all ministers, priests, and staff of the churches and buildings we visited for their warm and generous reception and for sharing so willingly their information and research materials;

George and Elizabeth Nicholson for their unflagging support (and especially to Elizabeth for her special expertise with maps); Mary-Grace Donnelly for finding the Mayer Studios in Munich, Germany; the Burton Library and the Fine Arts Department of the Detroit Public Library; Alan Botsford; Ordway Clifford; Jean Dodenhoff; Walter Buhl Ford; Winifred Fraser; Christine Klatt; Allen Konaszewski; Claudette McMeekens; David and Jennifer Morrison; Chris and Steve Moulios; Barbara Nicholson; Nancy Nicholson; Davison Pierson; Shirley Rogers; Jane Shoemaker; Bee Shiveley; Doris Smith; Sharon Snyder; Nicole Stroh; Peggy Thurber; Tena and Glen Winn; Rev. Harry Wolf of Trinity Lutheran Church; and all my tennis friends who have listened so patiently. I would also like to thank Burton Farbman, president of Farmstein Company, and Denise Tietze for their diligent though fruitless search for a photograph of one of the Tiffany windows in the Wayne County Building. The windows, boarded up during restoration of the building, could not be photographed, and we regret this important omission.

Introduction

Detroit

During more than two hundred years of settlement Detroit has lived under three flags and twice under British rule. For one reason or another, none of the changes in sovereignty brought about great growth in population, and Detroit was slow in growing even once it was safely back in American hands after the War of 1812. It took the introduction of steam navigation on the Great Lakes and the opening of the Erie Canal in 1825 to finally change Detroit from an outpost dependent upon the fur trade to a rapidly growing industrial city.

The newly increased population resulted in the development of several famous parishes between 1840 and 1880, and fine churches were built containing notable stained glass. It was, however, not until the late-nineteenth and early-twentieth centuries, when the need for workers in the automotive industry attracted thousands of immigrants from Germany, Poland, Ireland, Italy, Russia, the British Isles, and other parts of Europe, that Detroit really became the city of beautiful churches. The first thing immigrant families did, in a nostalgic link with their homeland, was build churches just like the ones they had left behind. They spared no expense to emulate in Detroit the beautiful stained glass windows that were part of their homeland memories.

The Medium of Glass

We call all glass "stained glass" when referring to colored glass windows. There are, however, several kinds of colored glass, and the following description may help toward a greater understanding of the complexity of stained glass and toward a deeper appreciation of its beauty.

The processes used to produce stained glass also distinguish the different kinds. There are four primary ways to color glass: pot metal, flashing, staining, and enameling. The first, pot metal, begins with a formula used to make white or clear glass—sand, soda or lime, and potash mixed and then melted in a clay pot in a furnace. The last two ingredients act as flux to assist the melting process. The glass is called metal when at nearly white heat the materials fuse and form liquid glass. The color in pot metal comes from adding various metal oxides to the clear glass mixture. Copper oxide produces blue-green; gold yields red or ruby; cobalt produces blue; manganese oxide produces purple; and iron oxide makes various greens or a bright yellow that is produced by reheating the glass after it has partially cooled. Impurities in these oxides lead to a very wide range of colors. Glass colored right through in this way is known as pot metal. The term probably derives from the addition of metal oxides to the pots of molten glass.

A second type of colored glass is called flashed glass. It is made by coating, or "flashing," white glass with a thin layer of colored glass. Flashed glass is more translucent than pot-metal glass, an advantage when a window's predominant hue is a deep ruby color. In the Middle Ages artisans etched away surface color with a sharp tool, and the etchings created an interesting effect. Today the process is accomplished with hydrofluoric acid.

A third coloring method is the one we usually think of first, staining. In this process, discovered early in the fourteenth century, clear or light-colored glass was painted with a preparation containing silver sulphide or chloride. When fired in an oven, the silver changes the glass to a yellow color. Subsequent stainings and firings can produce a deep orange.

Another coloring method, discovered in the sixteenth century, uses enamels. Enamels are compounds of ground glass and oxides that become fairly transparent when heated and fused to clear or white glass. Entire scenes can be painted in colored enamels on a single piece of glass. As the use of enamels became more widespread (during the seventeenth and eighteenth centuries) all the old methods of coloring glass—pot metal, flashing, and staining—were nearly lost. Colored enamels seldom have the brilliance of pot-metal glass but can take on a rich translucence when enamels are carefully applied. When poorly applied, they tend to flake with time and appear dull and heavy. Enameling fell out of favor in the late-nineteenth century as interest in the ancient stained glass techniques rekindled.

In addition to coloring, shaping plays an integral part in the production of stained glass. In the Middle Ages there were two methods for producing sheet glass, the muff and the crown process. Muff glass is made by blowing and swinging a bubble at the end of a pipe into a sausage shape. The ends are then cut off and the resulting cylinder split down its length, reheated and flattened out. The crown process, or spun glass, entails cutting a large spherical bubble off the blowpipe and attaching it by a daub of molten glass on its opposite side to an iron rod. It is then alternately reheated and spun until the centrifugal force of spinning opens it out into a flat circular sheet called a crown. There is no attempt to obtain uniformity of sheet thickness since variations produce desirable differences in color densities. These methods are still in use today.

Norman slab, or bottle glass, invented during the nineteenth-century Gothic Revival, is produced by a method rarely used today. A very uneven glass, it is made by blowing and molding a bubble of glass into a square mold, each side of which is then cut into a sheet of glass averaging about a quarter of an inch thick. The pieces are much thicker in the center than at the edges. This type of glass gives a deep, quiet radiance.

Regardless of the shaping method used the final step in all glassmaking is annealing, a process of gradual and controlled cooling. If not properly cooled, glass contains internal stresses that will sooner or later cause it to fly or crack. Poorly annealed glass is nearly impossible to cut. The annealer is usually a heated tunnel about seventy-five feet long with a moving track. The glass moves slowly down the tunnel about a foot a minute, cooling as it goes. Blowing, flattening, and annealing glass involve a lot of time, hardwork, and in some cases very expensive materials (gold and silver), so hand-blown glass is a costly "raw material."

Not all stained glass used in windows is hand blown. Dalle-de-verre, meaning glass flagstone, is a one-half to one inch thick modern cast glass (glass shaped in a mold) that made its first appearance in the United States in 1939 at the New York World's Fair. It is also called faceted glass and scab glass. Pieces of the cast glass are chipped or sawed into shape and arranged in a design with spaces between each piece of glass, then concrete is poured into the interstices between the glass. In recent years epoxy cements have replaced concrete. The technique is very different from leading, being more akin to mosaic. It produces strong panels, even sturdy walls, and some excellent examples can be found in Detroit.

One last type of glass requires passing mention. Cathedral glass, a commercial machine-rolled colored glass, is widely used in the United States. Despite its august name it should never be confused with handblown glass.

The principal purpose of any window, regardless of how it is made, is to admit light, and a good stained glass artist takes into account that his medium is a combination of colored glass and the light that actually passes through that glass instead of being reflected from it. Each piece of glass used should have a place in the total orchestration. Colored glass comes alive through its relationship with light and changes according to the seasons, the weather, and the time of day. A stained glass window may convey different moods at dusk or dawn than it does at noon. The vibrant hues of the blues and reds and golds glisten like jewels in direct sun, then merge into a general color when clouds appear in the sky. As dusk falls, the reds and yellows gradually fade until an evanescent blue is all that remains. It is a mystical experience.

The History of Stained Glass

Although vessel glass was made in very early times, window glass seems to have been a Roman invention. The Romans used cast slabs of glass about six inches square which were mounted in wooden frames. They do not appear to have used translucent colored glass. This, as well as the invention of lead strips to hold the pieces of glass together, seems to have originated in the Byzantine world, but exactly when, we do not know. Historians seem to feel that stained glass technique appeared sometime between 600 and 800 B.C. By the tenth century A.D. complex techniques of stained glass manufacture and the fashioning of stained glass windows had evolved, and the essential methods used have remained more or less unaltered to the present day.

Window making begins with the preparation of a sketch drawn to scale and rendered in watercolors. This is followed with a full-scale drawing, called a cartoon, of the window. The cartoon details the actual size and shape of each individual piece of glass; it also shows the lead line and metal supports. Patterns for the glazier (glass cutter) are made from this drawing, and he then cuts pieces of colored glass to the shape of the patterns. The segments are reassembled and the main figures of the cartoon are painted onto the glass. When details have been painted on the pieces of glass, they are fired in a kiln, permanently fusing the paint on the glass. (It should be mentioned that paint applied to matted or crosshatched areas become highly important as a means of controlling intensity of light in a southern exposure.) The artist next uses the pattern drawing as a guide in assembling the finished pieces of glass between strips of grooved lead known as cames. These bound leaded panes, or panels, are set into a metal armature. The armature is set into the window opening and fastened to iron bars, known as saddle bars, previously set in the surrounding stonework. In most cases, a stained glass window is actually a translucent mosaic held together by lead. The lead is not merely a connecting medium but in all good designs plays its own part by outlining main sections of the design and giving definition to the masses of color.

Stained glass window making reached an apex in the Middle Ages. Great churches and great cathedrals rose all over Europe, and they blazed with the color of stained glass. Except for the human features and folds of robes, all the color in medieval windows was in the glass itself. It is important to note, however, that painted glass originates with medieval glass. The figures in these windows were stylized, simplified, and bold and were derived from Byzantine mosaics and medieval manuscripts. The subject matter was religious and derived mainly from the Bible. These great storied windows were the teaching tools of the Church.

As the great cathedrals grew higher and higher in the fourteenth century, the windows became taller and narrower, often divided into lancets surmounted by tracery. Figures were elongated and elaborate arches and canopies filled the expanse remaining above the figures. Small scenes, sometimes secular in nature, were set in medallions and arranged up and down the windows. Another device for filling these huge windows was the use of a type of glass known as grisaille (the name derived from the French word meaning to paint or make gray), first introduced in the thirteenth century. The same black oxide commonly used for drawing was used to decorate windows of clear glass. The designs were often leaflike, and the motifs used became increasingly realistic. Also in the fourteenth century a silver stain was introduced, and yellow and green grew in popularity at the expense of the old favorites, blue and ruby. Heraldry was a subject in itself in the fourteenth century, and from this time onward the donor of a window often appeared as a figure in the picture.

The next change in style reflected the humanist influence of the Renaissance. The figures became flesh and blood, suffered and rejoiced, and expressed human emotions. Figures were set in perspective and, as in painting, realism became the ultimate concern of the artist. Renaissance windows were designed by painters and sculptors unfamiliar with the role of lead in glass designs, and these artists objected to leaded composi-

tions as being too crude for "modern styles." Thus, Renaissance artisans of the sixteenth century developed colored enamels, and these, coupled with silver stain and the old sepia enamels, allowed craftsmen to abandon completely the mosaic composition of colored pieces of glass bound together with lead. The traditional, idealized, didactic, and symbolic design and techniques gave way to windows filled with figures set in solid looking landscapes complete with buildings, skies, trees, birds, or set in interiors filled with their belongings and furniture. Stained glass of all kinds became less common as the Baroque and Rococo periods developed their dramatic, colorful, even gaudy interiors which required large clear windows.

In the seventeenth and eighteenth centuries the art of stained glass came close to extinction. During the Protestant Revolution and the Thirty Years War masterpieces from earlier centuries were destroyed. Lorraine's glass works, the major sources in Europe for the manufacture of pot metal, were totally destroyed in 1636, and by 1640 colored glass had become scarce and soon was virtually unobtainable. As the skills of creating stained glass declined, so the demand for it decreased and many existing windows fell into disrepair and vanished. The eighteenth century saw a renewed demand for figurative windows but now stained glass was thought of in terms of translucent oil painting. Lead and colored glass were used little by glass painters, who achieved color by using enamel paints. On the whole eighteenth-century enlightenment considered reason and plain daylight to be appropriate everywhere, even in church, and glorious old windows were even removed and dumped.

At first it looked as if the art of stained glass would be lost to the new world as well. The stained glass heritage did not cross the Atlantic with the early settlers mainly because the Puritans were among those who had destroyed stained glass windows in England because they believed them to be idolatrous. The Dutch settlers in America were, fortunately, not as fanatical as the Puritans and they replicated coats of arms in stained glass. These heraldic windows were the first stained glass images known to have been made in the thirteen colonies.

In the nineteenth century, the Gothic revival in architecture profoundly effected the art of stained glass. As Gothic architecture became increasingly popular, interest in the great medieval churches of England and Europe revived and a serious effort was made to discover the secrets of the radiance of medieval glass. In the United States the Gothic revival encompassed a wide variety of historical styles. Some artists chose to use the original medieval mosaic design with pot-metal glass, others used the Renaissance technique of painting with enamels, and some evolved a combination of both. During the post-Victorian era the light-transmitting qualities of stained glass were considered not as important as the imagery. These older windows are none the less admired for the luminescent quality of color and the vivid way in which characters are portrayed.

The search for the mysterious qualities of medieval pot-metal glass in the United States was diverted somewhat by the enormous popularity of two glass artists, John La Farge and Louis Comfort Tiffany. Both were painters of considerable stature who experimented with making opalescent glass, a milky glass of mixed streaky colors. Pictorially their work was stunning. Still, at least two other glass artists of the same era, Charles J. Connick of Boston and William Willet of Philadelphia, and the architect Ralph Adams Cram railed against opalescent windows and strongly advocated the return to pot-metal glass of the Middle Ages for the making of stained glass windows.

Even so, America's infatuation with nature in the nineteenth century made Tiffany famous, for he pleased America with his invention of landscape painting in glass. Although no home of the wealthy could be without them, landscape windows in churches was another matter as both Roman Catholic and Anglican churches have a long tradition of biblically inspired windows. Nevertheless, except for Roman Catholic churches, Tiffany landscape windows found their way into many worship places and Detroit boasts its share of these picture windows. Nineteenth-century America saw God in nature and so the acceptance of landscape windows in churches, even Anglican ones is easy to understand. Many studios, including Lamb Studios, America's oldest operational glass studio, quickly adopted opalescent glass and followed the lead set by La Farge and Tiffany. Opalescent glass even appeared in Classical revival architecture in America, revealing an obvious disregard for historical accuracy because, of course, no stained glass window ever adorned a Greek Temple.

Opalescent glass, called "American glass" in Europe, continued to be popular in the United States in the early twentieth century though it never really caught on in Europe. Then, when neo-Georgian styles revived in architecture, all stained glass became unfashionable for homes. (Frank Lloyd Wright, a notable exception, continued to design stained glass for his prairie houses.) Stained glass seldom went into commercial buildings after 1920 and only churches continued in its use. In the 1920s the clean lines and unadorned surface of the Bauhaus supplanted the floral elegance of Art Nouveau in public favor and Tiffany was passé. By 1930 he was forgotten and in the Great Depression the Tiffany Glass and Decorating Company filed for bankruptcy. The stained glass studios that did survive turned to the manufacture of plain glass.

Since World War II there has been a renaissance in stained glass. The churches' readiness to use famous artists such as Matisse and Chagall to design stained glass windows and the return of stained glass to its ancient role in architecture have combined to initiate some bold experiments in stained glass. No great modern works in stained glass have yet graced Detroit but worthy attempts can be seen in the clerestory of St. Paul Cathedral and in the Jewish synagogue Shaarey Zadek. Artists in stained glass now tend to work in a very personal figurative style, or entirely in abstract design. Others push for technical innovation. In the United States the self-contained panel has become a popular mode of expression in stained glass and such works are sometimes sold in art galleries in the same way as paintings.

I THE DETROIT INSTITUTE OF ARTS COLLECTION

It is little known that the European stained glass collection at the Detroit Institute of Arts is among the three most important in the United States. The richness of the museum's holdings provides an excellent background against which the nineteenth- and twentieth-century stained glass windows of Detroit's churches can be viewed.

The rise of stained glass to its status as one of the great art forms of the Middle Ages coincides with the development of the Gothic style in architecture in the twelfth century. The Detroit Institute of Arts is particularly fortunate to possess two examples of stained glass from the period of transition from the Romanesque style to the Gothic style in art. In addition to the panel from Soissons Cathedral, which is included in the guide-book, the Detroit Institute of Arts has on exhibition a rosette from Canterbury Cathedral that dates to the first years of the thirteenth century.

The museum's collection is distinguished for its quality and breadth. Virtually all important eras and countries are represented in the Detroit Institute of Arts, the single notable weakness being the lack of any important stained glass from the fourteenth century. The richest aspect of the collection is in German stained glass from the fifteenth and sixteenth centuries. In addition to the important dated panel from Boppard-am-Rhein (1444) and the Nuremberg *Crucifixion* (1514) which are included here, the collection includes the most magnificent sixteenth-century German windows in America. This consists of a series of five life-size standing saints from the area around Cologne of the first quarter of the sixteenth century. Other ex-amples of German stained glass on view in the museum include twelve fifteenth-century prophet panels installed in the Gothic chapel. One of the great achievements of stained glass in the Middle Ages is the advent of the silver-stained roundel. The small, unipartite panels are usually circular in shape. The collection of this material in the Detroit Institute of Arts includes examples by some of the most important artists in the medium.

The impact of the Italian Renaissance on the medieval tradition of stained glass is seen in the large *Nativity* (1517) from Cortona by Guglielmo di Marcillat. The panel of the *Town of Steckborn* (1661) is one of six outstanding Swiss pieces which show the development of European stained glass in the late sixteenth and seventeenth centuries, as the tradition was slowly abandoned in most of Europe.

The Detroit Institute of Arts Collection brings the history of stained glass into the modern era with panels designed by Frank Lloyd Wright and Henri Matisse. Wright's panel for the Darwin Martin House demonstrates the architect's desire to integrate the decorative arts with the architectural environment in a spirit akin to the role of stained glass in the Middle Ages. Matisse's *Wild Poppies* (1969) demonstrates the adaptability of the artist's late style, as seen in the paper cutouts, to stained glass windows.

Peter Barnet
Assistant Curator
European Sculpture and
Decorative Arts
Detroit Institute of Arts

TWO ECCLESIASTICAL FIGURES

French (Soissons Cathedral), 1205–1215
Gift of Lillian Henkel Haass
DIA 59.34; 73 cm × 74 cm
(Photo courtesy of the Detroit Institute of Arts.)

This panel, only recently identified as coming from the cathedral of St. Gervais and St. Protais in Soissons, is a rare surviving example of stained glass from the transitional period between the Romanesque and Gothic styles. The panel depicts a cleric holding a bowl in his left hand while he swings a censer with his right hand. He is followed by a cleric carrying a cross. The Detroit panel is substantially original. The significant areas of restoration are the head of the censing figures (a modern repainting), the drapery below the waist of the cleric with cross and the red Gothic window on the right of the panel.

In France, around the year 1200, Gothic architecture was beginning to mature. The development of medieval stained glass was intimately related to this new style of architecture. Gothic buttressing systems allowed thinner exterior walls, and walls seemed to disappear, replaced by great "curtains" of colored glass. The stained glass windows of the Gothic period are among the greatest artistic contributions of the Middle Ages.

The Soissons panel is an excellent example of the style and the technique of early-Gothic stained glass. Red and blue pot-metal glass predominates while the features of the faces and drapery are defined with dark gray pigment, demonstrating the graphic achievement of medieval glass painters.

The nineteenth century, particularly in the United States, saw an effort to revive the techniques of early-Gothic stained glass and to replicate its jewellike tones. We have some noteworthy windows in the churches of Detroit as glass artists like Charles J. Connick of Boston and Henry Lee Willet of Philadelphia deliberately rejected the painted window of the seventeenth and eighteenth centuries and returned to the pure colored glass, which they thought was the true medieval tradition. Examples in Detroit are the Willet windows in Trinity Lutheran Church and the Connick windows in Church of the Most Holy Redeemer. Many examples of ecclesiastical figures can be seen in the churches of Detroit, particularly the Polish churches of St. Florian, St. Josephat, and St. Stanislaus.

It is interesting to contrast this window with the sixteenth-century window of the *Nativity* (these works are located at either end of the entrance to the museum's Kresge Court) and to note the differences in the colors and the figures. The colors are brilliant in the medieval window and more subdued in the Renaissance window. The figures are bold in their stylization in the medieval window whereas the Renaissance window reflects the humanistic philosophy of that period in the realism of the figures portrayed.

THE THREE MARYS

German (Boppard-am-Rhein), 1444
Founders Society Purchase, Anne E. Shipman Stevens Bequest Fund
DIA 40.52; 58" × 29"
(Photo courtesy of the Detroit Institute of Arts.)

This panel of the *Three Marys* is part of a large and important series of stained glass windows from the Carmelite convent at Boppard-am-Rhein, south of Cologne. The church at Boppard has lost all of its medieval glass, and its panels are distributed throughout collections in Europe and in the United States. The Detroit panel is significant among these not only for its high artistic quality but for the date inscribed on the banderole held by the figure of God the Father at the top of the composition. The three female figures occupying most of the panel are the three holy women named Mary who witnessed Christ's Passion: their mournful attitudes are clearly conveyed here.

A number of the changes that took place in medieval stained glass between the transitional period of 1200 and the late-Gothic style of the mid-fifteenth century can be observed here. We see fewer small pieces of glass, resulting in fewer lead lines. The style appears less abstract and relies more on painted lines, less on the lead cames, for major design elements. In addition to using pot-metal glass, the window includes yellow areas created by the addition of a silver stain on the back of the glass. This is a yellow stain produced by laying a preparation of silver oxide or sulphide on the glass which is then fired, in contrast to the addition of metallic oxides in the molten pot-metal glass. This technique permits a great range and variety of effects.

The Passion of Christ was one of the most frequently depicted cycles in medieval and Renaissance glass and in later glass as well. Examples can be found in several Detroit churches, including: The Blessed Sacrament Cathedral; Christ Episcopal, Detroit; Christ Episcopal, Grosse Pointe; Christ Church Cranbrook; St. Paul's Roman Catholic, Grosse Pointe; and St. Florian, Hamtramck. St. Catherine of Siena itself depicts all the stations of the cross in stained glass in the clerestory.

THE CRUCIFIXION

German (Nuremberg), 1514
Artist: Workshop of Veit Hirschvogel the Elder (1461–1525); after a design
by Hans Suess von Kulmbach (ca. 1480–1522)
Gift of Mrs. Ralph Harman Booth
DIA 37.35; 18″ × 13½″
(Photo courtesy of the Detroit Institute of Arts.)

This small panel entitled *The Crucifixion* is one of the master-pieces of the stained glass collection at the Detroit Institute of Arts. It was made by the leading glass workshop in Nuremberg at the time, after a design by Hans Suess von Kulmbach—one of the great painters, draftsmen, and stained glass designers of the period. The Hirschvogel family painted the stained glass commissions of most of the leading artists of Nuremberg, in-cluding Albrecht Dürer, Hans Sebald Beham, and Kulmbach. We are fortunate to have a dated panel, in addition to the su-perb quality of the draftsmanship evident in this piece.

The composition of this Crucifixion scene is traditional in that the figures of Mary the Mother of Christ, and John the Baptist are portrayed at the foot of the crucifix. In the sixteenth century the draftsman's skill took precedence over that of the glazier. With Renaissance realism the body of the crucified Christ conveys intense suffering: the muscles are taut with ag-ony, blood spews from the lance wound on his right side, and the hands are clenched around the nails. Christ's body is ana-tomically realistic, no longer the stylized figure of the medieval period. The figures of Mary and John also are realistic, the folds of their drapery indicate that there is flesh and blood beneath, and their faces convey their anguish. It should be noted that John the Baptist is one of the most frequently depicted saints in Renaissance painting.

The Crucifixion, one of the last events in Christ's earthly life and part of the events collectively called Christ's Passion, is a popular theme, particularly in Episcopal and Roman Catholic Churches. All the Gospels agree that a number of women named Mary were present at the Crucifixion: the mother of Christ, the mother of James the Less, and Mary Magdalene. St. John's Gospel alone, however, indicates that he too was present and that just before Christ died, Christ commended his mother to John's care. Worthy depictions of the Crucifixion can be seen in Blessed Sacrament Cathedral, St. Paul's Episcopal Cathedral, St. Florian, St. Peter's Episcopal, Our Lady of Lourdes, St. Hyacinth, and Kirk in the Hills.

THE NATIVITY

Italian (Cortona), 1517
Artist: Guglielmo de Marcillat (1475–1529)
Founders Society Purchase, General Membership and Donations Fund
DIA 37.138; 8'10" × 66"
(Photo courtesy of the Detroit Institute of Arts.)

This window was made only three years after the Nuremberg *Crucifixion*. The two windows provide an excellent contrast. We see here the appearance of the High Renaissance style of Italy and southern Europe. (Actually, Marcillat was a French artist working in Italy.) The Nuremberg *Crucifixion* marks the end of the long medieval tradition of stained glass. Here in *The Nativity* we see a large stained glass window emulating the humanism of Italian Renaissance panel painting. The lead lines serve little of their former design function. The color is modeled and shaded like in oil painting, in contrast to the strong juxtapositions of solid areas of color in medieval glass. Only the facial features retain some of the draftsmanlike quality of medieval glass.

This window is a rectangular panel with Mary kneeling at the lower left. An ox and a donkey behind Mary are seen only from the shoulders forward, their bodies cut off by the edge of the panel. At the lower right is the infant Jesus flanked by two kneeling angels holding candlesticks. A standing male figure, Joseph, is behind the two angels. In contrast to the *Two Ecclesiastical Figures,* the figures in *The Nativity* are warmly human and emotion shows on their faces as they regard the child. Each of the members of the holy family has a nimbus. The scene is placed within a columned architectural setting that opens onto a landscape of green trees and plants. The colors of blue, red, green, lavender, and yellow are made less intense by the large expanses of sepia painting in the animals and architecture. The panel was ordered for the Cathedral of Cortona by Cardinal Silvio Passerini in 1517. There is a companion panel, *Adoration of the Magi,* in the Victoria and Albert Museum, London, England.

There are many Nativity scenes in the churches of Detroit. Noteworthy ones can be seen in the following churches: St. Boniface, St. Catharine and St. Edward, St. Cecelia, Annunciation, Nativity, St. Paul's Episcopal Cathedral, Trinity Episcopal, Christ Church Grosse Pointe, and St. Paul's of Grosse Pointe.

COAT OF ARMS OF THE TOWN OF STECKBORN

Swiss, 1661
Artist: Wolfgang Spengler (1624–after 1684)
Gift of George G. Booth
DIA 23.7; 17½" × 13¼"
(Photo courtesy of the Detroit Institute of Arts.)

The limited amount of stained glass produced in the seventeenth century was almost entirely heraldic in character. Most common among seventeenth-century Swiss secular panels are those displaying city coats of arms. The *Coat of Arms of the Town of Steckborn,* illustrated here, is a fine example. Usually the city arms were coupled with the personal device of the donor of the piece and flanked by standing heraldic beasts or figures—symbols of the town in which the glass originated. This particular panel depicts the arms of the City of Steckborn with ferocious lions rampant on either side of a circle containing crossed swords. A winged angel face sits atop the circle. A detailed map of the city is included in the upper portion of the panel. This panel is a tour de force that shows the technical achievements possible, including enameling, flashing, etching, silver stain, and grisaille. Secular panels produced in Germany and Switzerland in the sixteenth and seventeenth centuries contain the last vestiges of medieval style in stained glass. Their rich and brilliant color survives from the glass of the Middle Ages.

Other fine examples of heraldic shields and panels can be seen in the Edsel & Eleanor Ford House, in the Whitney House, at Cranbrook, at the Stroh Brewery Company headquarters, and in the churches Holy Redeemer, St. Stainislaus, and St. Andrew.

UNTITLED WINDOW FROM THE DARWIN MARTIN HOUSE

American (Buffalo, New York), 1904
Artist: Frank Lloyd Wright, 1867–1959
Founders Society Purchase, Dr. and Mrs. George Kamperman Fund and
*   Friends of Modern Art Fund*
DIA 71.8; 39¼″ × 26⅜″
(Photo courtesy of the Detroit Institute of Arts.)

This window is from the Darwin Martin House on Jewett Parkway in Buffalo, New York. The landmark house, now owned by the University of Buffalo, is being restored to architect Frank Lloyd Wright's original design. Wright, whose roots were in the nineteenth-century Arts and Crafts Movement, was modern in his rejection of historical styles. He was not, however, willing to give up the potential of stained glass and leaded panes. The scheme throughout the Darwin Martin House was complex, and each window in itself was an intricate design made up of numerous pieces of clear glass with scattered bits of stained glass held together by thin zinc or copper plated "leading."

The motif of the window shown here is a highly stylized version of wheat plants. The Detroit Institute of Arts owns one other window from the Darwin Martin House. It consists of two identical panes divided by horizontal and vertical leading into rectangles of various sizes. The main design element is a large arrow pointing upwards in the top two-thirds of the pane. The window is predominantly clear glass with scattered smaller areas of stained glass in yellow, green, and milky white.

In 1901 the *Ladies Home Journal* published Wright's plans and elevations for "A Home in a Prairie Town," officially heralding the prairie style. The Darwin Martin House is in this mode. Two-stories high, with a low, wide-eaved, hipped roof, the house is a study in horizontals. Wright subtly linked various units together: the main house with long banked windows, porches, the porte cochere, the gallery to the conservatory, and the terraced flower beds. The exterior is of stone and yellow brick. The exposed piers of vitreous brick within the house are an integral part of the decorative scheme.

THE WILD POPPIES

French, 1953
Artist: Henri Matisse, 1869–1954; window by Paul Bony, 1969
Founders Society Purchase, Robert H. Tannahill Foundation Fund and
*   Friends of Modern Art Fund; gift of Mrs. Allan Sheldon through*
*   the Elizabeth, Allan, and Warren Sheldon Fund and gift of Alice*
*   Kales Hartwick in memory of her husband Robert G. Hartwick;*
*   and Public subscription*
DIA 78.37; 33⅜″ × 137⅞″
(Photo courtesy of the Detroit Institute of Arts.)

The paper cutout for the window illustrated here was created by Henri Matisse in France in 1953, the year before he died. Paul Bony, also of France, translated the paper cutout into a stained glass window in 1969. The window consists of five panels, three of pot-metal stained glass separated by two panels with black crosshatching. Each of the three panels features a large dark blue flower on a diagonal, surrounded by leaves and fruits in greens, blues, oranges, red, and fuchsia; colors that are pure, fresh, and joyous. An alternate title for this work is *Pomegranate Blossoms,* possibly the more appropriate title because of the colors, and because it is said that the maquette was originally designed for a Dominican convent in Lyons, France. The pomegranate is a traditional religious symbol which alludes to the Church because of the unity of countless seeds in one fruit. It also symbolizes hope in immortality and in resurrection. In 1978 the Detroit Institute of Arts purchased the window and Matisse's colored paper cutout.

Matisse began to make cutouts of colored paper when he could no longer paint at an easel, and ultimately they became more than a simple substitute for painting. "To cut color makes me think of a sculptor's carving into stone," he wrote of his new art. Not until *Jazz,* his book on paper cutouts (1943–1944), did he recognize their potential as a means of expression in their own right: nor did he equate them with his painting until the 1951 dedication of the Chapel of the Rosary at Vence, France, for which he had provided paper cutouts with motifs based on traditional religious images, crosses, stars, palm fronds, and natural forms for the designs of the stained glass windows. The cutouts appear deceptively simple but the technique for creating them was excruciatingly exact. Matisse explained, "Sometimes the difficulties appeared: lines, volume, colors, were put together and then the whole thing collapsed, one part destroying another. . . . It is not enough to put colors against one another however beautiful: the colors also have to react to one another. Otherwise cacophony results. . . ." Those words echo the difficulties of great stained glass artists of all ages.

II CHURCHES

A NOTE TO THE READER

All directional descriptions of the churches are given according to the liturgical compass. The altar is always east and is the point of orientation for determining the direction of all other elements in the church, regardless of their true position on a regular compass.

Detroit was once known as the city of beautiful churches. Many of them still remain. They attest to the faith of the original French settlers and to that of later arrivals who were English speaking, German, Polish, Hungarian, Italian, Belgian, and many other nationalities. These people gave what they had or worked to raise the funds to make their churches as close to a little bit of heaven as they possibly could. The furnishings included glass for the windows, sometimes grisaille at first because it was less expensive, to be followed at a future date by great colored windows that transformed the interior of the church with each change in the light of day. Some of the finest stained glass in the United States is found in Detroit.

Detroit was Roman Catholic until 1816 except for sporadic Protestant services. In that year, at the instigation of Gov. Lewis Cass, the First Protestant Society, as it became known, was formed under the Presbyterian minister Rev. John Monteith. Five denominations were included, the Presbyterians, Methodists, Episcopalians, Baptists, and Congregationalists. As each left the First Protestant Society it built a church reflecting its own form of worship (and financial position). The early buildings of a congregation were usually simple structures, often favoring the New England meetinghouse style.

As Detroit grew in size and prosperity the churches became more ornate. Ethnic groups tended to engage architects of their own ethnic background, some having trained in Europe. Established architects from other parts of the United States also were hired to build churches in the prevailing style of the day. Detroit was fortunate in having several fine architectural firms of its own that made contributions to the churches and synagogues.

Gothic became the favored style in Detroit in 1836 because of the work of an Irish architect. Later in the nineteenth century this gave way to the Romanesque and still later to the Classical. Even the Venetian style can be found. Detroit is still the city of beautiful churches, memorials in brick and stone and glass.

Lucy Hamilton
Member, National Society of the
Colonial Dames of America
in Michigan
Co-founder, Church Tours in
Detroit with the Detroit
Historical Museum

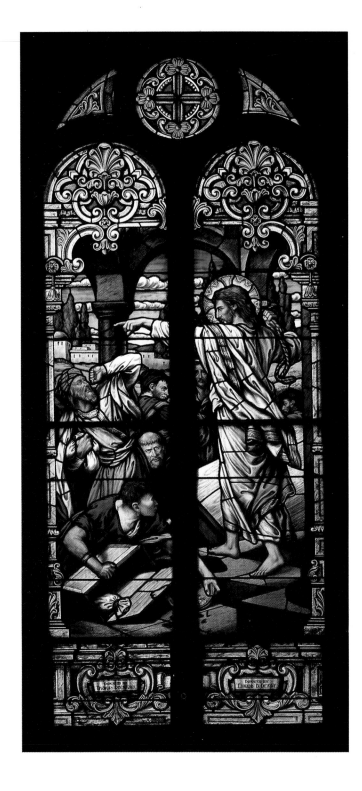

ANNUNCIATION ROMAN CATHOLIC

Address: 1265 Parkview
Architects: Donaldson and Meier, 1912
Window: The Cleansing of the Temple, north aisle of nave

The Cleansing of the Temple, illustrated here in a two-paneled window, tells the story of Jesus driving the money changers and merchants from the temple in Jerusalem. It is the only scene in the life of Christ that shows him in a violent mood, and it is rarely found in a window representation. St. John describes the scene in his Gospel: "And Jesus went up to Jerusalem and found in the temple those that sold oxen and sheep and doves, and the changers of money sitting: and when he made a scourge of small cords, he drove them all out of the temple, and the sheep and the oxen; and poured out the changers' money, and overthrew the tables; and said unto them that sold doves, Take these things hence; make not my Father's house an house of merchandise." The scene in this window is literally and dramatically interpreted by the glass artist and is painted in enameled glass in subdued colors of purples, green, blues, and sepia. The top of the windows are decorated with stylized flowers in yellow stain and the double panels are united by a small rose window with a cross in the center. Across the nave is another interesting window, also one seldom portrayed in church windows. It depicts the temptation of Christ by the Devil and Christ's dramatic refusal to be tempted by the Devil's offerings.

The windows of Annuciation Church are consistent in design and appear to be European, probably from a German glass studio. Around the altar, in stained glass, are the seven sacraments: Confession, Marriage, Ordination, Holy Communion, Baptism, Confirmation, and Extreme Unction. The aisle windows are scenes from the life of Christ: Annuciation, Nativity, Adoration of the Magi, the Boy Christ in the Temple, Baptism of Christ, Temptation by the Devil, Sermon on the Mount, The Cleansing of the Temple (shown here), Transfiguration, The Good Shepherd, Agony in the Garden, and also The Education of the Virgin. The rose window above the west entrance is a floral design in stained glass. The style is different from the other windows, and it may possibly be locally made.

Four hundred names were collected in 1906 and presented to Bishop John S. Foley with a request to establish a new parish. It was to include families in the area east of Burns Avenue to Connors Creek and north to Charlevoix Avenue. Bishop Foley consented and a parish was established on 1 May 1906. A lot was purchased on Bowen Avenue (now Parkview). Soon thereafter the old public school on Hibbard Avenue was put up for sale and the parish bought part of it and moved it to its lot on Bowen. It was a long, low frame structure and served as the church for the next six years. In June 1911 the present church was begun. The first mass was celebrated in the new church in June of 1912. It is Romanesque in style, of red brick with the brickwork forming a design on the facade. There are two short frontal towers. In 1985 the empty niche in the facade of the west portal was filled with a mosaic, made in Italy, depicting the Annunciation.

CASS COMMUNITY UNITED METHODIST

(Also known as Cass Avenue Methodist)
Address: 3901 Cass at Selden
Architects: Malcolmson and Higgenbotham, 1891
Window: Floral and Ornamental Window, north transept
Artist: Tiffany Glass and Decorating Company, ca. 1900

In the late-nineteenth century the popularity of the great land-scapists such as Frederic Church and Albert Bierstadt reached its height, and as could be expected this infatuation with nature was reflected in stained glass. The tradition of using only biblical themes in church windows gave way to a new flexibility in the United States, and landscape and ornamental windows found their way into the Protestant churches. Two of the finest examples are found in the north and south transepts of Cass Community Methodist Church. These windows are ornamented with pastel floral designs and sinuous fluid lines. The message lies primarily in their beauty. A Christian message, however, can be inferred by the choice of the flowers used in the two mandorlas of the central panel of the window. The passion flower for the Passion of Christ and the lily for the Virgin replace the figures of Christ and the Virgin traditionally found in mandorlas.

Two American painters, John La Farge and Louis Comfort Tiffany, began experimenting with glass in the 1870s and independently created a new form of glass, now called opalescent. The glass is noted for its streaky opal-like quality. Art Nouveau, a late-nineteenth-century style of decoration, was adopted and developed by Tiffany in the United States. It is characterized by the restless curving forms of its motifs such as ribbons, flowing draperies, swagged hangings, and its emphasis on plant life and art of the Near and Far East. The Cass Avenue Methodist windows are an outstanding example of Tiffany's Art Nouveau style. These transept windows were designed by the architects of the church, Malcolmson and Higgenbotham, and were executed by the Tiffany Studios of Long Island, New York. To our modern eyes these windows, unusual for Tiffany Studios, are more successful than his more popular opalescent "picture" windows which tend to be opaque and exclude light. The transept windows were listed as "Floral and Ornamental Windows" for Cass Avenue Methodist in a Tiffany Studio's pamphlet issued around 1910. The color of these floral designs, mostly in pot-metal glass, are pastel shades of pink, blue, lavender, green, and gold. The delicate leading is an integral part of the design, encompassing the pastel-colored glass in sinuous,

flowing lines. The mood created is one of a Persian painting. The simple Romanesque arches of the windows are divided into three large panels which are united at the top by two roundels. Romanesque churches of the early Middle Ages in Europe, with their small windows, had little or no stained glass, but historical accuracy did not deter architects of the American Romanesque revival style from filling their large rounded windows with stained glass if they so desired, or, more likely, if their patrons did. The windows in the narthex of the church and in the west front carry the same decorative motif as the transept windows and could be by the Tiffany Studios or by another studio completing the overall design.

Cass Avenue Methodist is one of several churches designed by William G. Malcolmson and William E. Higgenbotham in the Romanesque revival Style. (Another one is the Church of the Holy Rosary on Woodward at the Ford Freeway [I-94].) The architects received their training in the offices of local architects, but their major influence was the Richardsonian Romanesque, a modified Romanesque revival style developed by the nationally famous American architect, Henry Hobson Richardson. The exterior of Cass Avenue Methodist presents a medieval effect with its heavy limestone masonry and massive tower at the corner where the streets meet. There is fine sculptured detail over the rounded arches of the doorways. The interior of the church is in the form of a modified Greek cross and the ceiling beams, as well as the furnishing, are of oak. 39

CATHEDRAL CHURCH OF ST. PAUL

Address: 4800 Woodward at Warren
Architects: Ralph Adams Cram, Goodhue, and Ferguson, 1911
Windows: First Day of Creation, first bay of clerestory, south nave
Artists: Donna Swanson Taylor, J. and R. Lamb Studios, New Jersey

The stained glass in the clerestory of St. Paul's Episcopal Cathedral is quite different from the stained glass in the rest of the church, so different that one may experience a sense of shock on first seeing it. These windows representing the First Day of Creation are part of a series of thirty-six windows in the twelve bays of the nave clerestory. They are abstract in design and interpret the first day according to Genesis, "Let there be light." Progressing from darkness to light, the windows interpret the days symbolically as they lead one's eyes to the high altar. St. Paul's Cathedral is the first of the historic churches in Detroit to experiment with contemporary design.

The architect, Ralph Adams Cram, proposed a plan for the completion of the stained glass, and essentially the program has been carried out. That is, all but for the clerestory, where he had suggested that the windows depict thirty-six saints with appropriate scriptural verses. In the late seventies it was decided that the clerestory was too high for anyone to appreciate the saints suggested by Cram, and the decision was made to employ bold symbolism rather than detail. The feeling emerged that there should be a series of windows memorializing the Old Testament. Ideas were solicited in an open competition, and Donna Swanson Taylor, a member of the parish, won. She worked closely with the J. and R. Lamb Company of New Jersey to ensure faithfulness to her concept. These pot-metal glass windows are bold and rich in color, portraying on the south side the six days of Creation and on the north side symbolic representations of the Old Testament figures Noah, Abraham, Moses, David, Isaiah, and Jonah. The windows are successful, for they allow ample light, the main function of the clerestory.

In the rest of the cathedral the general scheme for the stained glass is based upon thirteenth- and fourteenth-century glass in France and England. There is a generous use of medallions and panels. By far the greatest amount of glass work has been designed and executed by Heaton, Butler, and Bayne of London, England, and Charles J. Connick of Boston. The chief exception to this is the window that was formerly in the chancel of Grace Church and was moved to Grace Chapel in the north transept of the cathedral. It was executed by the Franz Mayer Company of Munich, and is a window of brilliant coloring and life-size figures representing the visit of the Magi.

Practically all the stained glass in the chancel and transepts together with the north nave, comprising a dozen windows, is the work of Heaton, Butler, and Bayne. Among these windows is the magnificent five-lancet chancel window known as The Passion. This window is a memorial to Theodore H. Eaton, Jr., who was senior church warden for twenty years. There are four scenes in each lancet, and some of the best modern stained glass work attainable in modern times re-creates the fourteenth-century atmosphere felt in the medallions and panels. Deep blues, purples, greens, and ruby red are its powerful colorings. The clerestory windows of the chancel are by the same studio, as is the rose window in the west front of the cathedral depicting the figures of the Four Evangelists.

Connick's work in stained glass is noted for its brilliant colors, rich symbolism, and abundant use of scriptural passages. Five nave windows were designed by Connick, all of them memorial windows. The Edwards window, dedicated to the son of a former dean of the church, memorializes the young man's courage and sacrifice, as he was killed in World War I. The others are the two Hannan windows and the Borgman and Fletcher windows.

Also significant are the twelve Spanish windows evenly distributed to the left and right of the sanctuary. They are of sixteenth-century glass and came from a Spanish cathedral. Some of the saints figured in the windows are the well-known Mary Magdalene; Augustine; James the Great, who was the patron saint of Spain; and John the Baptist. A number must be of local interest, though, for they are difficult to identify.

The present building of St. Paul's is the congregation's third, built from 1908 to 1911 and consecrated in 1919. Designed in thirteenth-century English Gothic style, the cathedral is acclaimed one of architect Cram's best works. The tower designed for the crossing has yet to be built, but once it is constructed, the soaring lines of the cathedral will reach their climax. Its absence, however, in no way detracts from the cathedral's magnificent interior with its huge columns, carved oak woodwork, Pewabic tile floors, and beautiful stained glass windows.

CATHEDRAL OF THE MOST BLESSED SACRAMENT

Address: 60 Belmont at Woodward
Architect: Henry A. Walsh, Cleveland, 1913
Window: The Holy Name Window, north transept.
Artist: Willet Studios, Philadelphia

The window illustrated here is a revival of the so-called worship of praise windows found in many of the great cathedrals of Europe. Its five tall lancets fill the north transept. The Willet Studios spent more than a year creating this window. The upper portion of the central lancet pictures Christ enthroned and clothed in ruby red, red being the symbol of power and martyrdom. Above him God is pictured in purple (symbol of God the Father) and green (symbol of the triumph of life over death), surrounded by angels. God is infrequently pictorialized; instead he is usually symbolized by a hand. Beneath Christ in his royal robes are angels and saints. In the two lancets on either side of Christ are the holy men on one side and the holy women on the other reaching out to Christ. John the Baptist and St. Joseph are the figures closest to Christ and St. Joseph bears the budding rod, symbolic of Christ's origin. At the apex of the holy women is the Virgin Mary with the sword of sorrow piercing her heart. In the two extreme side lancets musical angels protect heaven from evil. Cherubs and religious symbols fill the traceries above. Below the main window are five predellas. The center one shows Christ during his temptation in the desert. To Christ's right is Goliath, giant of the Philistines, who was slain by David for blaspheming the Holy Name. To the right of this (although partially obscured) are the Psalmist singing praises to the Holy Name, Hannah teaching young Samuel to pray, and Sidrach, Misdach, and Abdenago praising God in the midst of the fiery furnace into which they have been thrown for refusing to blaspheme the name of God. To Christ's left Jeremiah, prophet of the Old Testament, weeps at the spectacle of the daughters of Israel worshipping a golden calf. To the left of this are Noah and his family offering sacrifice to God after leaving the ark. They are surrounded by a rainbow, symbol of God's convenant with man.

Seventeen large medieval-style stained glass windows by Willet Studios, all composed of pot-metal glass rich in jewellike colors of ruby, amethyst, emerald, and sapphire, grace the church. Each window depicts a scene in sacred history from the birth of Christ to the Pentecost.

The church, which now serves the Archdiocese of Detroit as the Cathedral of the Most Blessed Sacrament, was originally planned as a parish church to serve the people of the Woodward-Boston Boulevard area. In 1913, the first pastor, the Reverend John Connolly, began the construction of a permanent church building. The original contractor was John Finn and Company of Detroit.

The building, in Norman Gothic style, has 136-foot twin towers on the west facade (completed by Diehl and Diehl in 1951), and a graceful, slender spire, or *flèche,* over the crossing. The exterior facing is of Ohio sandstone with Indiana limestone used for buttress facings, traceries, and doorways. Gothic flying buttresses support the outer walls of Our Lady's Chapel. Stone groined vaults and tall clerestory windows, replete with tracery and stained glass, enhance the interior of the building.

CENTRAL UNITED METHODIST

Address: 23 East Adams at Woodward
Architect: Gordon W. Lloyd, 1867
Window: The Great West Window
Artist: Willet Studios, Philadelphia, 1955

Central Methodist's original stained glass windows, grisaille in nature, were imported from England. Because the windows had been damaged over an almost ninety-year history, a major change was planned, and the Willet Studios of Philadelphia were invited to design and execute new stained glass windows for the entire church. All the windows, including The Great West Window illustrated here, were dedicated in 1955. These windows follow the tradition established in the stained glass windows of the Gothic cathedrals of medieval England and France, a tradition that allowed stained glass artists to interpret religious themes using the familiar decorations and symbols of the particular era in which they lived.

The subject of the great seven-lancet traceried window in the west facade—"I am come that they might have life, and that they might have it more abundantly"—is represented in contemporary terms. In this window Christ is symbolized by the heroic figure of a young beardless man striding across the three central lancets. The forces of evil and disaster are shown in the three left lancets: women and children slaving under poor working conditions; the door to employment being closed to blacks, Jews, and foreigners; a lynching in a small inset. Above this the free voice of the church is being stopped by the forces of the totalitarian states, communism and fascism. Next a mother is holding in her arms a son killed in the field of battle while many wounded and mutilated by war are shown lying on their beds of pain. The terrific blast of the atomic bomb can be seen. All these represent the forces of evil that we know at the present time.

To the right of Christ are symbols of the more abundant life available in the United States today. The great forces of nature are shown being harnessed to the dam from which comes the power of electricity for the use of the farmer and others. Next is the free pulpit where man's religion can be proclaimed without fear and a Red Cross and a doctor innoculating the young athlete, symbolizing free education and health for all; also shown is a refuge for those of foreign birth or foreign ancestry, the Japanese-American Hostel. Industrial problems are shown being solved at the conference table with labor and management sitting down together to work out their differences. Pictured also is the free ballot for men and women, white

and black. At the bottom is the Statue of Liberty welcoming displaced people from foreign lands, and the depiction of an ocean liner being loaded with supplies of food and clothing for those in need across the sea. The United Nations building in the lower right hand corner is symbolic of political cooperation, and in the tracery above the figure of Christ is the seal of the World Council of Churches. In the four small tracery openings are the symbols of Courage, Faith, Love, and Loyalty. In the two large tracery openings are symbolized the Crucifixion and the Resurrection.

The subject matter of all the windows in the church is the life and teachings of Christ. The Great West Window is the church's largest because the congregants face it as they leave the church, and it therefore requires a more discernible impact than the windows contemplated during services. All the other windows of Central Methodist are executed in the Gothic style of miniature scenes in medallions. Clockwise from the altar and above the gallery are windows depicting the Nativity, teaching, the Passion, and the Resurrection. Clockwise from the altar on the main floor are windows depicting the Baptism, children, parables, Christ blessing children, ministry, miracles of healing, and the Last Supper. All these windows are three-lancet traceried windows depicting the main subject in medallions and predellas depicting related scenes. These windows are of pot-metal glass with a minimum of painting, jewellike colors, and are in the medieval style of the thirteenth and fourteenth centuries.

In 1864, after a disastrous fire in the church building on Congress Street, a splendid stone edifice was built at Woodward and Adams. It is Gothic in style, being a blend of both English and French Gothic. A dramatic event occurred in the history of Central Methodist when in 1935 the State of Michigan set timetables for the widening of Woodward Avenue from Adams northwards. In order to save this beautiful church from demolition, a thirty-foot section between the transept and the front of the church was removed so that the church front and the 180-foot tower could be moved back. This was accomplished without so much as disturbing the pigeons in the tall tower, or so they say. It was a remarkable engineering feat.

45

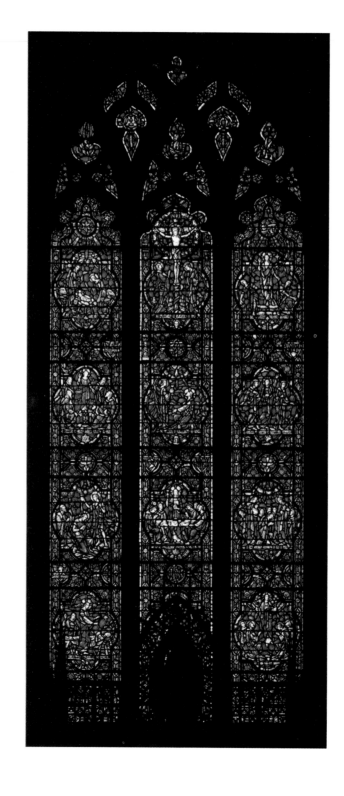

CHRIST CHURCH CRANBROOK

Address: 470 Church Road at Lone Pine, Bloomfield Hills
Architect: Bertram Grosvenor Goodhue Associates, 1925–1928
Window: The Life of Christ, east window
Artist: Nicola d'Ascenzo, Philadelphia

The east window, illustrated here, depicts in twelve medallions, scenes from the life of Christ. Starting in the upper left corner downward the episodes are: the Nativity; the boy Jesus' discussion with the doctors; the Baptism; and raising the dead at Nain. The center panel starting at the bottom upward depicts: washing of the apostle's feet (obscured by a screen); the Last Supper; the garden of Gethsemane; and Calvary and the Crucifixion. The upper right hand corner reading down shows: the Resurrection; the road to Emmaus; Whitsunday; and the Ascension. Above, in the tracery are symbols of God the Father, God the Son, and God the Holy Spirit, and two crosses with the letters alpha and omega, the first and last letters of the Greek alphabet symbolizing the beginning and the end. At the base of the window, although obscured here, are a bride and groom, the donors of the window. The inscription reads: "This window is erected in joyful remembrance of September 27, 1924, whereon Carolyn and Henry Booth were united in Marriage." The window is in fourteenth-century medieval style with scenes in small medallions and the donors of the window featured at the bottom. Nicola d'Ascenzo, who designed and executed the window, was one of the advocates of the use of antique glass in the style of the great medieval churches of Europe. (Another example of his work is the Great West Rose Window of St. Cecelia Church, Detroit.) All the stained glass windows in Christ Church, except for one in the baptistry, were designed for the church and installed between 1925 when ground was broken and 1928 when the building was consecrated. The glass was made by several different studios, but all follow the same medieval style.

In the narthex a window shows St. Barbara, born in the third century A.D. of a rich, heathen father who isolated her in a tall tower—hence her attribute the tower. She was converted to Christianity nonetheless, but when her father learned of it he became so enraged that he struck off her head. After committing this awful deed he was killed by a bolt of lightning amidst a great crash of thunder. Because of her father's thunderous punishment, St. Barbara has become the patron of artillery, soldiers, gunsmiths, and firefighters.

Christ Church's large west window is dedicated to womankind and depicts hundreds of famous women throughout history from saints to suffragettes. The baptistry window by

J. Gordon Guthrie shows John the Baptist baptizing Jesus. The other window in the baptistry has two medallions, the lower one of the presentation of Christ in the Temple and the upper medallion of the three Marys at the tomb, and is attributed to the thirteenth century, Amiens, France. The five clerestory windows in the nave executed in grisaille glass are by G. Owen Bonawit. In the Chapel of St. Paul, the windows, designed and made by Toland Wright of Cleveland, depict the life of St. Paul, Apostle to the Gentiles. The Chapel of St. Dunstan, patron saint of artists and craftsmen, is dedicated to all who labor with their hands. The windows represent the arts and crafts and were executed by Wright Goodhue. The Chapel of the Resurrection also has windows by Goodhue, showing the three archangels: Gabriel, herald of the Last Judgment; Michael, the fighter of evil spirits; and Raphael, guide of men.

Christ Church Cranbrook, its rectory and sextonry, were built during the years 1925 and 1928 and the church school from 1937 to 1939. The church is English Gothic in style, and the exterior is of Ohio sandstone. The sextonry is of the various native stones of Oakland County. A tower to the southwest of the church houses the carillon. On a clear day the view from the top of the tower embraces Lake St. Clair and the Detroit skyscrapers. The buildings, complete with furnishings and the original endowment, were the gifts of Mr. and Mrs. George Gough Booth of Bloomfield Hills.

47

In memory of Henry Francis
1837   While

Le Hunte Lyster the beloved Physician and the first
aligned with you I sought light rather than

friend of many little children
darkness · 1894 ·

CHRIST CHURCH–DETROIT

Address: 960 East Jefferson
Architect: Gordon W. Lloyd, 1863
Window: Lyster Window, baptistry
Artist: Franz Mayer and Company, Munich, Germany, 1905

Suffer the Little Children to Come Unto Me, better known as the Lyster Window, is a memorial to members of the Lyster family. William Narcissus Lyster, the first rector of Christ Episcopal Church, was born in Ireland and attended the University of Dublin. He immigrated to Detroit as a Protestant minister. After he left Christ Church he founded several missions in the area now known as the Irish Hills, a name he gave the location because it reminded him of his native land. An interesting detail in the history of the Lyster window is that photographs of members of the family were sent to the Mayer Company in Munich to have the likenesses incorporated into this window; thus, the faces, with the exception of Christ, are all recognizable likenesses of members of the Lyster family. The older man on the left is the minister himself and the man next to him is the physician, Dr. Francis Lyster, who, with his family, donated the window. Although the inclusion of the figures of the donors in a window was a common practice beginning in the fourteenth century, examples in Detroit are quite rare, and the Lyster window is the only one known to include an entire family.

The window is typical of Mayer windows of the late-nineteenth and early-twentieth centuries, a style one easily recognizes in many of the historic churches in Detroit. This window has three lancets, a landscape background, and life-size figures heavily painted in enamel with rich colors and architectural canopies above them. The leading in this style is no longer important. What is important is the presentation of a three-dimensional landscape scene with recognizable figures.

Among the church's other notable windows is The Great West Window depicting the life of Christ. On the left are scenes of the prophecies from the Old Testament that predict the birth of Christ. Dominating the lower part of the window is the Last Supper, and above that the Crucifixion.

St. Michael's Chapel in the north transept contains windows that are fine examples of English stained glass by Clayton and Bell, London, England, and depict St. Michael, St. George, Eunice (the Jewish mother of the apostle Timothy), and St. Elizabeth, the mother of John the Baptist. The six clerestory windows by J. Wippell & Co. of Exeter, England, depict the six parables of Christ. On the south side there are The Good Samaritan, The Prodigal Son, and The Lost Sheep and Lost Coin.

On the north are The Wise and Foolish Virgins, The Man with Talents, and The Last Judgment. The narthex contains two signed Tiffany windows, one a Resurrection angel and the other an Ascension angel.

In the south transept a Tiffany window portrays one of the legends of St. Elizabeth of Hungary. St. Elizabeth was the daughter of the King of Hungary and, as an infant, was betrothed to Ludwig, son of the Landgrave of Thuringia and Hesse. At an early age she was sent to live at the Wartburg Castle, the home of her betrothed's family, in order to be trained in the local ways. The castle was on a high hill and it was difficult for the poor and infirm to climb the steep path to receive their ration of bread. Elizabeth, noting this, filled her apron with bread each morning and took it to the foot of the path. To make trouble Ludwig's jealous brother reported what Elizabeth was doing. One morning in the middle of winter, Ludwig confronted Elizabeth on the path and asked what she was carrying. When she opened her apron it was filled with roses. The legend is depicted here with Elizabeth in an enchanting garden. No sign of winter is visible. This landscape garden window is a beautiful example of Tiffany's work. However, the opalescent layered glass does not fulfill the window's function of admitting light. Rather, it is a delightful picture in glass.

Christ Episcopal Church parish was organized in 1845 by members of St. Paul's parish. Their first church was a small one built on the present site. In 1860 a new chapel was erected and used while the old church was torn down and the new one constructed. This interim chapel still stands behind the present structure. The church that can be seen today was consecrated in 1863. It is Gothic revival in style, based on the European Gothic style of the early fourteenth century. The exterior is of native gray limestone trimmed with dressed sandstone. In the interior there are transepts with galleries and a roof supported by graceful hammerbeam trusses. The woodwork is all local butternut except the roof. The distinctive and massive arcaded belfry dominates the west facade. In it are the oldest set of church bells in the City of Detroit. They were cast in Philadelphia and installed in 1863.

49

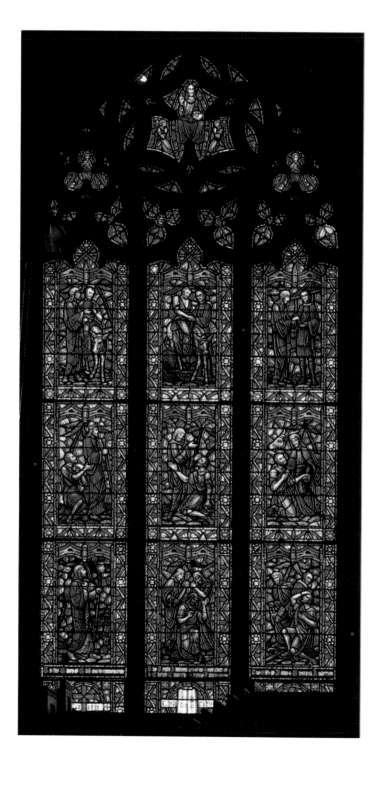

CHRIST CHURCH GROSSE POINTE

Address: 61 Grosse Pointe Boulevard, Grosse Pointe Farms
Architects: Mayer, Murray, and Phillip of Bertram Grosvenor Goodhue
Associates, New York City, 1930
Window: The Good Samaritan, west window

The west window of Christ Church Grosse Pointe, illustrated here, depicts the parable of the Good Samaritan from the Gospel of St. Luke. It is divided into nine panels with three quatrefoils above and is executed in a combination of Gothic colors of greens, blues, reds, and yellows. Depending upon the kind of day and position of the sun, different colors predominate. On a sunny morning the yellows and reds are outstanding, while on a cloudy day or later in the afternoon, the window appears to be predominantly blue and green. The story of the Good Samaritan is told simply in picture-book fashion as it would have been told in the Middle Ages for people who could not read. Starting with the lower left hand corner and reading from left to right: a man going from Jerusalem to Jericho; the man is set upon by thieves; the man is robbed and left wounded. Center panels left to right: a priest passes by the wounded man; a Levite passes by the wounded man; a Samaritan gets down from his own beast to help the wounded man. Upper panels from left to right: the Samaritan sets the man on his own beast and gives him something to drink; the wounded man sits on the Samaritan's beast beside the innkeeper; the Samaritan gives two coins to the innkeeper to take care of the wounded man, saying "take care of him, and whatever you spend, I will repay you when I return." The predellas (partially obscured here) contain, from left to right: Faith with a cross; Charity with the Bible opened to St. Luke; and Hope with an anchor. The center quatrefoil above depicts the figure of Christ attended by two angels, and the smaller quatrefoils each contain worshipping angels. In medieval fashion the window is composed of pot-metal glass in strong colors and possesses a flat appearance without perspective that gives an ethereal, mystical feeling, rather than a sentimental or humanistic one. The figures are stylized representations in simple lines with little detail.

All the windows in the church are executed in the medieval style and, because they were designed and installed in a relatively short space of time, there is a unity in the size of figures, subject, and color although not of studios. The eight nave windows and the two transept windows, telling the story of the life of Christ, were made by the Willet Stained Glass Company of Philadelphia. Henry Lee Willet personally chose the pot-metal glass and Norman slab glass used in the windows.

Represented are the Annunciation, the Nativity, the boy Jesus in the Temple, the Baptism, the Sermon on the Mount, the wedding feast at Cana of Galilee, Peter's confession of faith, Christ's washing of the disciples' feet, the Last Supper, and the Resurrection (the latter two are located in the north transept). The east window, designed by Clement Heaton of London, England, and executed by the De Raniere Studios of Detroit, represents the coming of the Holy Spirit, or Pentecost. The two double-lancet windows in the south transept, also executed by the De Raniere Studios, present various saints with their attributes: St. Cecelia with the harp, St. Catherine of Alexandria with a spiked wheel, St. Elizabeth of Hungary with an apronful of roses, and St. Margaret of Antioch with a sword. Several gemlike windows from the Connick Studios of Boston grace the stairways to the gallery and undercroft. Other smaller windows designed in medieval style are in the baptistry, the narthex, and the gallery.

Christ Church Grosse Pointe was the fifth mission started by Christ Episcopal Church, Detroit. The groundwork for the church was laid as early as 1923 when Sunday school classes for Grosse Pointe children were held in several Grosse Pointe homes. In 1928 the cornerstone of the church proper was laid. The building, English Gothic in style, was originally designed as the chapel of what was planned to be a much larger edifice. The narthex was patterned after the Chapter House at Wells Cathedral in England, the cloister inspired by that of Canterbury Cathedral in England. The sandstone for the exterior of the church was quarried in Clearville, Pennsylvania, and was selected because of its iridescence in sunlight. Gray limestone from Indiana was chosen for the inside. In December 1930 the opening service was held. Christ Church was officially admitted to the diocese as a parish in 1947, and in 1950 was consecrated. Noteworthy in the interior of the church is the reredos, handsomely carved in oak, by craftsmen of Mowbray's, London, England. It depicts the three principal scenes from the life of Christ: Nativity, Baptism, and Ascension. The choir stalls, pulpit, and the lecturn also exhibit superior wood carving.

CHURCH IN THE CITY
(ORIGINALLY FIRST UNITARIAN)

Address: 2870 Woodward at Edmund
Architect: Donaldson and Meier, 1890
Window: The Good Knight
Artist: John La Farge, 1899

The First Unitarian Church, now the Church in the City, once contained four large stained glass windows by John La Farge. Three of them, above the west entrance, were removed when the church was sold to the Church of Christ in 1934. The three were subsequently given to the Detroit Institute of Arts where they now await restoration. The fourth La Farge window, The Good Knight, illustrated here, remains in the church, a memorial to Judge Albert Grenville Boynton, a police justice in Detroit from 1873 to 1878.

The influence of La Farge's first trip to Italy in 1894 is clearly reflected in the classical balance and symmetry of this window which is reminiscent of an early-fifteenth-century Florentine sculptural niche. The figure, dressed in fifteenth-century Tuscan burgher's costume and cap, is shown removing a shield from the left arm and holding a sword. In the base of the window are the coats of arms of the Alden and Boynton families. The inscriptions read, "In memory of Albert Grenville Boynton," followed by a quotation from Edwin Arnold's *Death in Arabia,* "In enlarging Paradise lives a life that never dies. When ye come where I have stepped ye will wonder why ye wept." In the wreath at the top of the window are the dates 1837 and 1898. Except for the face, hands, and inscriptions, this window is made entirely of pot-metal and opalescent glass. To create the semblance of marble and architectural forms in the window, La Farge selected mottled and streaked glass whose colors were appropriate to the subject. Opalescent glass admits less light than pot-metal glass or most enameled glass. Therefore the architects flanked this window with two diamond-patterned, slightly tinted windows that afford light and brighten the interior of the church.

In the late-nineteenth century, Greek temples, Roman baths, and Renaissance palaces were faithfully replicated throughout the United States. The one exception to the historical accuracy of these copies was that many of them contained stained glass windows. Part of the popularity of stained glass may be explained by the client's predilection for it and his indifference to historical accuracy. Thus it is no surprise to see nineteenth-century opalescent windows by La Farge in this Romanesque revival church.

The First Unitarian Church (sold to the Church of Christ in 1934 and bought by the Church in the City in 1984) was remarkable for its severely simple design even before it was altered in 1936 when Woodward Avenue was widened. The gabled front on Woodward Avenue relied for its effectiveness on the rich texture of its masonry which stood out in contrast to the deep shadows of a starkly plain Romanesque porch. A small round turret at the front of the church and a square tower at the rear added further interest. The porch was disfigured by alterations during the widening of Woodward Avenue.

CHURCH OF THE MESSIAH

Address: 231 East Grand Boulevard at Lafayette
Architect: Calvin N. Otis, 1852
Window: Annunciation/Visitation/Adoration of the Magi, north nave

The two-lancet window, illustrated here, depicts three separate scenes in the life of the Virgin. At the top is the Annunciation with the kneeling archangel Gabriel, holding a lily, his symbol as well as that of the Virgin. He is announcing to the Virgin her Immaculate Conception. Above the Virgin is the Holy Spirit in the form of a dove. The middle scene is the Visitation. It depicts the visit of the Virgin Mary, already with child, to her cousin, Elizabeth, who had learned from the archangel Gabriel that she would give birth to John the Baptist. Below this, the Adoration of the Magi, which represents the visit of the Magi, wise men from the East, bearing gifts of gold, frankincense, and myrrh for the newborn baby. Tradition has given the names of the Magi as Caspar, Melchoir, and Balthasar. Their gifts have symbolic meaning: gold to a king; frankincense to one divine; myrrh, emblem of death, to a sufferer. (Frankincense is an aromatic gum resin, burnt as incense; myrrh, a gum resin used in perfumes and medicines.) The figures in the window are housed in architectural canopies and are monumental and realistic, the style popular at the turn of the twentieth century. The scenes are painted in enameled glass in subdued tones of brown, green, red, and yellow. The liberal use of silver stain allows light to penetrate the window. The two predellas contain a design of stylized architecture.

The stained glass windows in the Church of the Messiah represent different studios, and except for one, the studios that made them are unknown. The stained glass window in the north nave, depicting the Boy Jesus in the Temple, is by the Mayer Company of Munich, executed in 1904, and typical of their late-nineteenth-century style. All the windows are in the pictorial Renaissance style of the late-nineteenth and early-twentieth centuries. They are heavily painted in enamel on glass and are rich in color with monumental figures. The Good Samaritan window in the north aisle is a memorial to Zina Pitcher, a physician known as the father of Detroit schools. His studies on American Indian materia medica were a classic in his day, and it was largely he who was responsible for building the department of medicine at the University of Michigan. Across the church there is a memorial to Levi Bishop. This man was a tanner and shoemaker by trade until he lost his right hand after

an accident (Pitcher performed the amputation). In the American tradition of self-reliance Bishop took up law and became very successful. He wrote poetry and translated from French into English numerous historical works pertaining to the settlement of the northwest. The law department of the University of Michigan was established during his tenure as regent.

The parish of the Messiah started as a mission of Christ Church, Detroit, in 1874 at East Jefferson and Mt. Elliot, then Hamtramck. The present church building, originally St. Paul's Church, was formerly located at Congress and Shelby Streets and had not been used by that parish since 1894. It was given to the mission of the Messiah for the cost of one year's taxes on the old site. It was moved stone by stone in 1901 to the corner of Lafayette and East Grand Boulevard where it became the Church of the Messiah; the stained glass windows were moved along with the church. The firm of Stratton and Baldwin executed the move from Congress and Shelby to its present location. The church exterior is of gray limestone with an asymmetrical facade and corner tower. Basically the church was still in the style of the New England meetinghouse, the only change being the substitution of Gothic for Georgian motifs. The interior of the building is unobstructed by columns or galleries and is spanned by large hammerbeam trusses. The very fine carved wood reredos, with the unusual feature of sculpture in the round, was added at a later date as was the Pewabic tile floor in the chancel.

55

FIRST CONGREGATIONAL CHURCH OF DETROIT

Address: 33 East Forest at Woodward
Architect: John Lyman Faxon, 1891
Window: The Great Round Window, north transept

The architect John Lyman Faxon spent considerable time in Europe studying Romanesque and Byzantine architecture before designing the First Congregational Church. His studies roused his interest in the Romanesque wheel window, the earliest form of the rose window. The window shown here is a version of the wheel window known as an Italian *occhio* (the Spanish equivalent is called *ojo de buey,* or bull's eye). This type of window differs from the more common rose window, where the emphasis is on the pattern of interlocking stone tracery, in that it is devoid of stone tracery. The glass panels in such windows are supported by ironwork that radiates from a central point or is arranged in vertical and horizonal bars.

The windows of First Congregational Church are perhaps Detroit's only example of the Italian *occhio*. The pattern of the *occhio*, illustrated here, is delicately leaded circles of white glass. In the center of the large circle is a leaded cross. The ironwork spokes point to twelve smaller circles of white glass, each one centered with a small stained glass star. Outside the large circle, and between the spokes of the wheel, are twelve brightly colored stained glass "eyes." The emphasis is on the number twelve (a favorite number in Christian symbolism), twelve divisions in the large circle, twelve smaller circles radiating from it, twelve "eyes," and stands for the twelve apostles, and in a more extended meaning, occasionally represents the entire church. Below the large occhio window, five round-arched windows, the number five for the five wounds of Christ, carry out the pattern of delicately leaded circles of white glass. The south transept windows are similar to the one illustrated and allow for the penetration of plenty of light to emphasize the details and decorations of the interior of the church.

The Congregationalists in Detroit were affiliated with other denominations until 1844, at which time they began to hold their own services in the Old City Hall on the east side of Woodward Avenue on Campus Martius. The following year they built their own church at the southeast corner of Jefferson and Beaubien. Several years later they built yet another church on the southwest corner of Fort and Wayne (now Washington Boulevard). They remained there until 1891 when the population of the city began to move north on Woodward Avenue. It was then that First Congregational built its present church at Woodward and Forest. The church, an adept blending of elements drawn from the Romanesque and Byzantine styles of Italy and Dalmatia, is constructed of rock-faced red sandstone and the exterior is dominated by a tall campanile with slender arcades. Atop the cap of the tower is the archangel Uriel who is associated with light. Numbers were ascribed symbolic meanings in the Middle Ages, and Faxon incorporated these meanings into the facade of the church. A low porch with a series of five large Romanesque arches, five for the five wounds of Christ, extends across the facade of the building at the entrance level on Woodward Avenue. Five smaller arches are repeated above, and above that seven still smaller arches, seven, the symbol of charity, grace, and the Holy Spirit. At the top of the facade are three windows, symbolic of the Trinity and also the number of completion in the Romanesque and Byzantine worlds.

The interior of the church is in the form of a Latin cross. The sanctuary bears a striking resemblance to the lower church of St. Francis of Assisi in Assisi, Italy, while some of the details and ceiling decorations are similar to those in its upper church. The decorations of the barrel vaults are patterned after ceiling mosaics in the Tomb of Galla Placidia at Ravenna. Decorations on the transept arches reflect those found on the arch in the apse of San Vitale at Ravenna. The abundance of color, an essential element in Byzantine art, is made prominent by its overall use and by the light from the carefully designed windows.

57

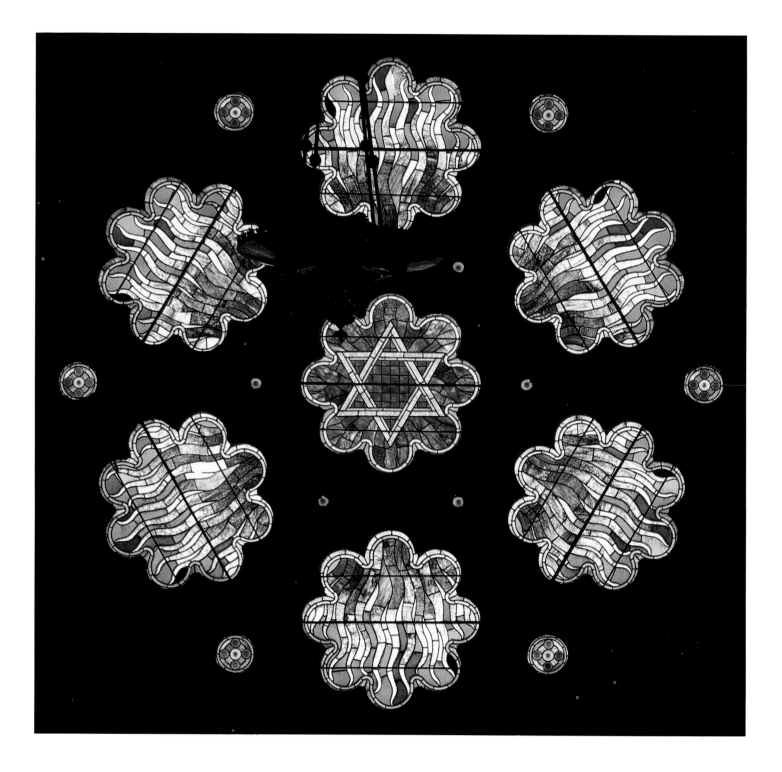

FIRST PRESBYTERIAN

Address: 2930 Woodward at Edmund Place
Architects: Mason and Rice, 1899
Window: Flames of Fire, Woodward side of sanctuary

This window (partially obscured by a hanging lamp) is unique in Presbyterian churches because of its inclusion of the Star of David in its center. The Star of David denotes that Christians look at Bethlehem as the City of David and the birthplace of Christ. The flames in the window represent the Holy Spirit and symbolize Pentecost and the birth of the Church. According to tradition Mary, the Apostles and others were gathered together in a house in Jerusalem following Christ's Ascension. Suddenly there came a sound from heaven as of a rushing, mighty wind that filled the house. Then appeared the cloven tongues like fire and entered into each of them. They were filled with the Holy Spirit and began to speak with other tongues as the Spirit moved them. The flames in the window also recall the Burning Bush, an image from one of the best-known stories about Moses. While tending the sheep of his father-in-law, Moses saw a bush that was burning with fire but that was not consumed. When he paused to look at the bush God called to him out of its midst. It was then that Moses heard that he was chosen to return to the land of the Pharaoh and lead the Israelites out of Egypt into the Promised Land. The window, while not a true rose window, gives the appearance of one. The six rosettes containing the flames are set in a circle and are a mixture of pot-metal and painted glass. The flames leap outward. Each is bordered by eight scallops in blue glass. The flames are dark brown, lightening to a cream color at the tips and the background is green pot-metal glass. The central rosette containing the Star of David is bordered in deep yellow stained glass. The interior of the star consists of red mosaiclike squares of pot-metal glass, and the periphery is brown glass. The effect is dramatic.

There are several interesting windows in First Presbyterian. The Good Tidings Window above the center balcony commemorates the premiere sermon of the church's first minister, John Monteith. In 1816 the Reverend John Monteith, fresh out of Princeton Theological Seminary, was induced to come to Detroit by a group of civic leaders headed by Governor Lewis Cass. Monteith took over the ministry of the Protestants which Father Gabriel Richard had largely undertaken along with his own Catholic ministry. In 1817 a university was founded by Monteith and Richard which eventually became the University of Michigan. Monteith was appointed president at a salary of twenty-five dollars a year and Father Richard served as vice president at eighteen dollars a year.

Another interesting window, also above the center balcony, shows John on the Island of Patmos writing the last book of the Bible, Revelation. This is a Tiffany window though not typical of what we consider Tiffany style. The Jesus in Sorrow Window to the right of the altar was given as a memorial in 1911. It is also a Tiffany window but in the layered glass and pictorial style usually associated with Tiffany Studios. The St. Paul Window in the church house hallway was designed by D'Ascenzo, a well-known designer of glass in Philadelphia, to depict Christianity being taken to the cities of the New Testament world by the Apostle Paul. The tower windows in the sanctuary are filled with shaded blue glass. This admits light and at the same time encourages a contemplative mood in the interior of the building.

The architects of First Presbyterian church, Mason and Rice of Detroit, were inspired by Henry Hobson Richardson's Romanesque revival church, Trinity, in Boston. Enormous masonry arches support a massive tower as in Trinity, but in Detroit rock-faced red sandstone has been used as building material instead of granite. The present building, the third for the First Protestant Society of Detroit (legal name for the First Presbyterian Church), was erected in 1899 with the church house being added in 1911. The interior of the church is in the form of a Greek cross, the shallow arms lending themselves to a concentric arrangement of pews. When Woodward Avenue was widened in 1936 the handsome triple-arched entrance porch with its interesting marquetry and stone carvings was shifted to the southern facade on Edmund Place.

FIRST UNITED METHODIST CHURCH

Address: 1589 West Maple at Pleasant, Birmingham
Architect: Andrew Morison, 1952
Window: The Music Window, Music Room
Artist: Henry Lee Willet, Willet Studios, Philadelphia

The three-lancet window illustrated here was designed to indicate the role music has played through the ages in the service of religion. Depicted throughout the tops of the three lancets (partially obscured on the right) are angels playing various types of ancient instruments. In the top portion of the central lancet is the figure of Christ holding a chalice (obscured here); the smaller figures of some of the apostles surround him. The Gospel of Matthew (26:30) describes the specific incident represented here, when Christ instituted the Sacrament of Communion at the Last Supper after which he and the apostles sang a hymn and went out onto the Mount of Olives. It illustrates the essential part music has played in church worship from earliest times. The two lower panels of the central lancet contain further references to music in biblical times: Miriam, sister of Moses, accompanying herself on a timbrel, and singing a song of thanksgiving for the deliverance of the Israelites from Egypt; David the Psalmist, kneeling with his harp. The Psalms, which he wrote, are an integral part of many worship services today. The left lancet pictures composers of some of the hymns used in the Methodist worship service: Martin Luther, Giovanni Palestrina, J. S. Bach, and John Wesley. The right lancet illustrates the music service of First Methodist Church: the organist, choir mistress, and the junior and senior choirs.

A unified iconography for the complete stained glass fenestration of First Methodist Church was designed by the architect, Andrew Morison, and the glass artist, Henry Lee Willet. The windows represent the more modern designs of the Willet Studios typified by the use of large pieces of glass and simplified forms to blend with the newer architecture. The pot-metal glass in these windows is dominated by the primary colors—blue, red, and yellow. The series presents a panorama of the creation of the universe and man. It comes to a climax in the great rose window located above the balcony that depicts the twelve disciples commanding the worshipper leaving the church to go out into the world and preach the gospel to every creature. The themes represented in the windows, beginning at the west end of the north nave are: Creation, the Ten Commandments, the prophets, the Nativity, the Invitation, preaching, praise, bap-

tism, prayer, marriage, Communion, the Resurrection, Christ and the children, the parables and miracles, and Christ in the workday world. Flanking the Invitation Window in the chancel, the Four Evangelists are represented by their symbols, winged man for St. Matthew, lion for St. Mark, ox for St. Luke, and eagle for St. John. The Children's Chapel window portrays Old and New Testament scenes of children in the Bible. The small rose window in the Runkel Chapel depicts the Crucifixion. The chapel is named in honor of Arnold F. Runkel, Minister Emeritus.

First Methodist is built of brown brick with white sandstone trim. In style it is modified English Gothic. An interesting feature of the church is that there are 369 doors opening to the various rooms of the church—the sanctuary, the chapel, the pastor's study, Fellowship Hall, the nursery, and many classrooms. The doors represent Christ's invitation to man to enter and be saved. The first church building in Birmingham was of the Methodist denomination. Built by a congregation established in 1821, the wooden structure erected in 1839 was located at the corner of Merrill and Bates. In 1873 a brick Methodist church was built at the corner of Maple and Henrietta. When the First Methodist congregation celebrated its one hundredth anniversary in 1921, the entire community participated. Twenty-five years later the congregation, realizing that larger facilities were needed, adopted the slogan "Now we shall build again." By 1950 the cornerstone of the present church was laid and the church was consecrated in 1951. Today the First Methodist church complex is set on nine acres of landscaped and wooded land.

FORT STREET PRESBYTERIAN

Address: 631 West Fort at Third
Architect: Albert H. Jordan, 1855
Windows: Grisaille Nave Windows

Grisaille glass has been used in churches over the centuries to glaze windows until more costly stained glass could be afforded. The nave windows at Fort Street are all grisaille. The congregation must have wished to retain the light glass because it provided more illumination to the interior of the church, which was darkened by polished black walnut furnishings. Grisaille, a thirteenth-century development named for its gray appearance, is comprised of a delicate pattern painted on clear glass with a thin gray or black line, and then fired. The paint itself was a mixture of copper oxide or iron oxide (which lent the mixture its black, brown, or gray-green color), pulverized glass (which allowed the paint to fuse with the surface of the window glass when the pane was fired), and a binding agent such as a mixture of wine and gum arabic, from the acacia tree. The technology has changed little today. Toward the end of the thirteenth century artists began inserting small colored panels or medallions into the grisaille glass. Fort Street's triple-lancet windows are bordered with pot-metal stained glass of either abstract or plain design. Stained glass also fills the traceries. The leading in the windows is diamond shaped, and the delicately etched grisaille patterns vary in theme with each window. Of slightly tinted glass, the effect of the windows depends upon light and design rather than on figures and color. Good grisaille windows are rare because so many have been replaced; thus, Detroit is fortunate to have such fine examples as the windows of Fort Street Presbyterian Church. Other windows of note in the church are the rose window behind the organ pipes, the stained glass window above the balcony, and the stained glass windows in the narthex.

Fort Street Presbyterian dates its beginnings to 21 February 1849 when it was organized as the Second Presbyterian Church. In 1855 it moved into its present building and changed its name to Fort Street Presbyterian. Albert H. Jordan, an Englishman, was the architect and he incorporated designs borrowed from buildings in England into Fort Street Presbyterian Church. (James Anderson, a draftsman in Jordan's office responsible for much of the work, went on to be the architect of Old City Hall.) The building is Victorian Gothic in style. Notable is the well-proportioned corner tower ending in a graceful spire which rises 230 feet above the street. The church is constructed of limestone from the quarries at Malden, Canada. The roof is supported by large timbered hammerbeam trusses, second only in size to Westminster Hall in London, England. Pewabic tiles representing various ecclesiastical crosses are included in the tile floor of the aisleways and narthex. The building is now one of Michigan's historical landmarks as it is the oldest Protestant congregation in Detroit still worshipping at its original location.

HOLY CROSS

Address: 8423 South Street
Architect: Henrik Kohner, 1924
Window: The Assumption of the Virgin, south transept
Artist: Ludwig von Gerichten, Columbus, Ohio, 1927

The Assumption of the Virgin, the window illustrated here, is a mixture of pot-metal and painted enamel glass. The design is in Renaissance style with large realistic figures that would have been familiar to the Hungarian immigrant congregation of Holy Cross. The Virgin in her traditional blue robe is carried heavenward attended by two angels bearing her attributes, lillies and a palm branch. She is poised on blue sky and protected by billowing white clouds. Radiating from her head is a nimbus of golden rays. The Gothic architecture above her contains stylized floral patterns, and the two predellas below have architectural designs containing a cross radiating heavenly light and a crown bearing the twelve stars of the apocalyptic vision. With the exception of Christ, no other figure in Renaissance art is as frequently portrayed as the Virgin Mary. This window and all the stained glass windows in the body of the church were designed and executed by Ludwig von Gerichten in 1927.

The five enamel-painted sanctuary windows, installed when the church was built, were designed and executed by the Detroit Stained Glass Works. Flanking the crucified Christ in the center panel are St. Peter and St. Paul. On either side of them the windows contain figures of the Hungarian saints of the House of Arpad, Saint Emerich, Saint Ladislaus, Saint Elizabeth, and Saint Margaret. These windows were designed in the Renaissance style using heavy enamel painting. The von Gerichten windows complement these earlier sanctuary windows installed in 1924.

Hungarians came to Detroit in four time periods. The end of the nineteenth century saw the first significant number of Hungarians settling in Delray, then an independent suburb of Detroit. The second sizable immigration came after World War I and was composed of refugees from territories separated from the homeland. A third group of political refugees came after World War II, and the fourth and final group was heroes of the 1956 rebellion against the Communists. The first two groups founded the church community. Their first church, a frame building, built in 1906, stood on the site of the present school building. The present church, a twin-towered red-brick Gothic revival building was built in 1924. The architect, Henri Kohner, born in Temesvar, Hungary, was both the architect and the builder. The interior of the church is noted for its murals, the Mysteries of the Holy Rosary, which Andras Dauber an artist of Hungarian descent was commissioned to paint in 1948. He completed them within the year. The murals, together with the stained glass windows, are outstanding features of the church.

HOLY FAMILY ROMAN CATHOLIC

Address: 641 Chrysler Drive (I-75 service drive) at Lafayette
Architect: Van Leyen and Schilling of Detroit, 1910
Window: L'Immacolata, south aisle

This round-arched window shows the Virgin of the Immaculate Conception in all her glory as Queen of Heaven. Her royal blue robe is encrusted with gold chains, stars and rings—gold the symbol of pure light. The elaborate gold crown signifies her royalty, the stars encircling her head are the twelve stars of the apocalyptic vision. Stars also symbolize her title "Stella Maris," Star of the Sea. Further tribute to her role as Star of the Sea is the string of fish festooning the hem of her robe, and the small and large ships at her feet. The fish is also a symbol of Christ, a symbol, therefore, of the child she had conceived. Her foot stamps on the head of a green serpent crushing out evil; and heads of cherubs gaze up in adoration. She stands between two Corinthian columns. Above her in the round arch of the window is a design of stylized roses, symbol of Mary as a "rose without thorns." In the predella is a frieze of grapes, symbol of the Blood of Christ; peaches, the fruit of salvation; and the pomegranate, the hope of resurrection and immortality. The window is heavily painted in Renaissance style, with an emphasis on the colors of deep blue and gold.

The remaining stained glass windows in Holy Family Church are painted in the same Renaissance style in dramatic rich colors. The clerestory windows of ca. 1980 represent the Ascension, Christ triumphant, Isaiah, the Annunication, the expulsion from the Garden, the Good Shepherd, Gethsemane, Pentecost, and St. Cecelia. The aisle windows which date from 1910 represent the Pietà, St. Joseph, the Immaculate Conception (shown here), San Vittore, San Giovanni Battista, the Sacred Heart, Santa Monica, St. Michael, San Pietro, and the expulsion from the Temple.

The parish of Holy Family was organized in 1908 as the mother church of the Italian people in Detroit. The first Italian immigrants to Detroit in any sizable number were Lombards from a town near Milan in 1880. The later and heavier influx at the turn of the century largely came from southern Italy and Sicily and they founded the parish. The parish used the chapel of Sts. Peter and Paul Church as a place of worship until its own church was completed in 1910. Although the parishioners no longer live in the neighborhood of the church, Holy Family remains the mother church of the Italian population of Detroit. The church is seventeenth-century Italian Baroque in style, a reminder of their native land. The side altars reflect the predominantly Sicilian origins of the early parishioners; the one to the left of the high altar is dedicated to Our Lady of Trapani and the one to the right to Maria de Ferrasini. The main altar, side altars, and communion rail are of imported Carrara marble. The basilica-type interior consists of a nave and side aisles with large rounded columns.

HOLY REDEEMER CHURCH

Address: 1721 Junction at West Vernor
Architect: Donaldson and Meier, 1922
Windows: The Resurrection and the Raising of Lazarus, north aisle
Artist: Charles J. Connick, Boston, 1922.

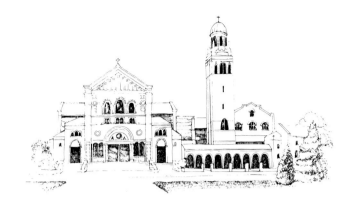

Charles J. Connick of Boston designed and executed all the aisle windows of Holy Redeemer Church. He designed these double-lancet windows in medallion style, a method used in the fourteenth century. The center medallions of the windows illustrated here depict the Resurrection on the left and the Raising of Lazarus on the right. Each window consists of three medallions, the center one carrying the story. The top and bottom medallions in both windows contain a cross, one of the oldest and most revered of all symbols. The figure of the resurrected Christ and the two angels in the left medallion are in white glass, dramatically set against the brilliant colors surrounding it. The right medallion, depicting the figure of Lazarus, also in white glass, contrasts with Christ, cloaked in ruby red, as he raises Lazarus from the dead. Around the medallions are borders featuring stylized leaf and flower designs and geometrical shapes. Connick's richly colored glass in tones of blue, red, green, purple, and yellow, and his use of pot-metal glass in jewellike designs can be seen in these aisle windows. The windows transform and control the light entering the church and are true stained glass windows in the medieval tradition, not painted pictures on glass.

The twelve two-lancet windows in the north and south aisles are designed in the same fashion as the windows illustrated. In the south aisle the central medallions tell the stories of six of Jesus' parables, and the north aisle medallions reproduce the story of his life and miracles. The clerestory windows are by the Detroit Stained Glass Works, those in the transepts and around the altar are by an unknown designer. In the north transept there is an heraldic window with the Stars and Stripes and the nation's motto, "E Pluribus Unum."

The order of the Most Holy Redeemer, known to us as the Redemptorists, was founded by St. Alphonsus Maria de Liguori in 1732 in Italy. Since that date it has served missions all over the world. The Redemptorist Fathers served Old St. Mary's from 1844 to 1872 and from 1890 to 1893. In 1880 they set about establishing a parish in Springwells, a western suburb of Detroit, now a part of Detroit proper. The Fathers took possession of a large stretch of sand and turned it into the largest parish in Michigan. The first services were held in a rented two-story building, commonly referred to as Paddy McMahon's saloon. However, by the end of 1880 a small frame church was built on the site of the present church and a Redemptorist named Brother Thomas was the architect. For many years the little church was known as "The Little Church on the Sand Hill."

The present red-brick church and accompanying buildings were designed in 1922. The church is in basilica style based on the Church of St. Paul in Rome. The campanile, or stone bell tower, was built between 1924 and 1927 in memory of the young men of the parish who died in World War I. Father Aegidius Smulders, the founder of the parish, was a missionary and a former Confederate Army chaplain. Although mustered out from a defeated army, at the age of sixty-five he still had the strength and vigor to establish the Church of the Most Holy Redeemer.

IN·LOVING·MEMORY·OF
·JOHN·G·KEIL·

IROQUOIS AVENUE CHRIST LUTHERAN
Address: 2411 Iroquois at East Vernor
Architect: Louis Keil, 1913
Window: Easter Window, chancel

A floral design of Easter lilies fills the chancel window, illustrated here. The design and stained glass are a direct descendent of the Arts and Crafts Movement that flowered in Detroit between 1886 and 1906. This movement advocated the return to the hand-crafted work of the artist. The origins of the movement are traced back to England when the Pre-Raphaelites banded together in 1848 with the express goal of improving the condition of the arts in that country. They revolted against what they considered the tawdriness and shoddiness of the mass produced goods of the Industrial Revolution. Their desire was to return to the beauty and simplicity of the Middle Ages. The ancient formulas of medieval glass were reconstructed and pot-metal glass was used once again for stained glass windows. The simply designed window illustrated here is an example of this movement. The pot-metal glass in colors of blue, green, and white are strong and clear and the leading is an integral part of the design. The lily is symbolic of purity and the Resurrection and, therefore, the window is known as the Easter Window. Other examples of handcrafted art glass can be seen in the narthex of the church.

The remaining windows in Christ Lutheran are large windows with figures painted in Renaissance pictorial style which was popular in the late-nineteenth and early-twentieth centuries. In addition to the Easter window illustrated here, the chancel contains a Nativity window in this style. Clockwise from the altar the other windows represent the Crucifixion; the Resurrection; Jesus calling Peter and Andrew to the Apostate, saying "Follow me, and I will make you fishers of men"; Peter's failed attempt to walk on water after his boat capsizes; the An-

gel (God's messenger to the people); God's word (represented by the lamb and the cross of St. Paul, the sword of the spirit, and a cup symbolizing communion); "Suffer the little children to come unto me," (a biblical scene of Christ blessing children from Matthew 19:13–15); the Sermon on the Mount; the Good Shepherd; and Gethsemane.

The congregation of the Iroquois Avenue Christ Lutheran Church was organized in April of 1911 and commenced worship in a rented church on Canton Street at Kercheval Avenue. It soon purchased the corner lots on Iroquois and Waterloo Street, now East Vernor, as a site for its future church. In In 1911 the parsonage was built. It was designed by architect Louis Keil and built by Henry C. Marlow, both members of the congregation. In 1913 Keil and Marlow teamed up again to design and build the present church. The dominant characteristic of the architecture of Christ Lutheran is clearly Gothic, but it is a typically eclectic building of the early-twentieth century with influences from the Arts and Crafts Movement. The addition of a parish house, designed by the firm of Beckett and Akitt, was completed in 1928.

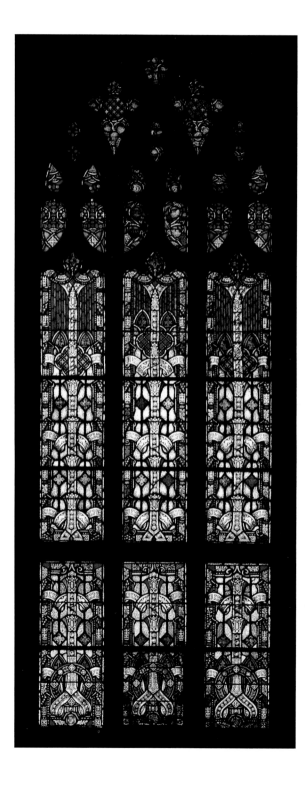

JEFFERSON AVENUE PRESBYTERIAN

Address: 8625 East Jefferson at Burns
Architects: Smith, Hinchman and Grylls 1925
Window: Decorative Clerestory Window
Artist: Willet Studios, Philadelphia

The ten windows of the clerestory are decorative windows in the fashion of the one illustrated here. Each window has three lancets united by fine tracery above. These windows are green and yellow in tone with decorative patterns of scrolls, grapes, and vines. Highlighting the green and yellow and making those colors more intense by contrast are flashes of deep blue, purple, red, and pink. The tracery openings contain deeply hued stained glass and continue the decorative patterns. These windows are not typical of the Willet Studios but are more in the manner of the Art Nouveau movement, with its emphasis on nature and sinuous, flowing lines, that was popular in England and the United States in the 1920s.

More typical of the Willet Studios is the large west window over the entrance that is done in the medieval style in which the figures are stylized representations, the lines simple with little detail, and the windows possess a flat appearance without perspective. It is easy to recognize these large Willet windows composed of small panels and alive with details of biblical stories. The west windows of Trinity Lutheran and St. Catherine of Siena come to mind. The huge west window of Jefferson Avenue Church is in three sections; the lower one shows Christ's birth, the middle, his ministry, and the top, his Resurrection. The predominant colors of this window are intense blue, red, and purple and shed a bluish-rose light on the nave. It is disappointing that the full effect of this magnificent window cannot be fully felt because of the heavy Plexiglas panel protecting the outside which, though necessary in today's troubled times, does impede the light. It is startling to let one's eyes wander from the deep subdued tone of the west window to the bright greens and yellows of the clerestory which are light and joyful in spirit. The aisle windows which are small and narrow continue a decorative pattern with colors more intense than those above.

It is interesting to note that in 1855, when Detroit numbered only about twenty-two thousand people, three large Presbyterian churches were under construction: Fort Street Presbyterian, First Presbyterian's second building (located on State and Farmer), and Jefferson Avenue Presbyterian (located on Jefferson Avenue between Russell and Rivard). The latter congregation moved to Jefferson Avenue and Burns in 1926 where it had built the present large Gothic style edifice with its pointed arches, buttresses, and stained glass windows. The present church is made up of two distinct units, the large auditorium and the Dodge Memorial Chapel. The Memorial Chapel also contains Willet windows, but these were completed at a later date than those in the sanctuary. While also jewellike in color and medieval in design these windows differ in the presentation of their figures as the artists reflect the styles of their own times.

Jefferson Avenue Presbyterian is a perfect expression of the Arts and Crafts Movement that revolted against the tawdriness of mass-produced articles, emphasizing once again handcrafted work with detail carefully and lovingly done. In the first sermon given in the new church, Samuel H. Forrer, the pastor, expressed the sentiments of the movement in his "Message of Truth." He stated, "No church should reflect the dishonesty of using material in an attempt to deceive the eyes of the worship of God, there should be no shams, no imitations. Let everything be true, real, and genuine." To this end the builders had searched the world for pure materials and handcrafted articles; granite from New England, bells from England, organ from Boston, furnishings from Chicago, windows from Philadelphia, marble from Italy, copper from Colorado, lead and zinc from South America, and vases from Japan. All the wood carvings in the sanctuary were done by the Anton Lang Family of Oberammergau, Bavaria.

73

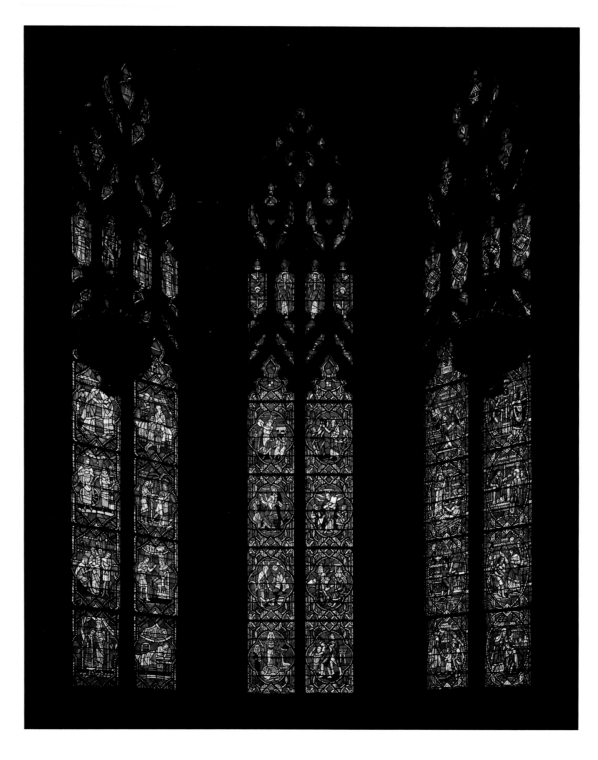

KIRK IN THE HILLS

Address: 1340 West Long Lake Road, Bloomfield Hills
Architects: Wirt Rowland and George D. Mason and Company, 1958
Windows: The Moses Window, The Joseph Window, and The Samuel
  Window, Melrose Chapel
Artists: Joseph G. Reynolds and Wilbur Herbert Burnham, Boston

Surrounding the altar in the Melrose Chapel are nine double-lancet windows portraying great figures of the Old Testament along with outstanding events in their ministries. The three center windows of these nine are illustrated here. Moses, the central figure in the Old Testament, is pictured in the middle window, which is over the altar. All the stained glass windows in the church were designed and executed by two Boston firms: Joseph G. Reynolds and Associates, and Wilbur Herbert Burnham. Both firms designed The Moses Window. To the left of The Moses Window the story of Joseph is portrayed in a window designed exclusively by Reynolds; to the right is the story of Samuel in a window designed by Burnham. The windows are executed in fourteenth-century medallion style and the primary colored pot-metal glass is patterned after glass in Chartres Cathedral, France. The story begins at the lower left of the Moses and Joseph windows and reads across the double lancet from left to right. The Moses Window depicts: Moses in the bulrushes; Moses and Aaron visiting the afflicted; Moses and the burning bush; Moses and Aaron pleading with the pharaoh to liberate the Israelites; Moses' hands being stayed; Moses and the Ten Commandments; Moses' anger at the people for their worship of the golden calf; and the serpent of brass. The Joseph Window on the left of Moses represents: Joseph and the coat of many colors; Joseph's dreams and visions; Joseph sold into Egypt; Joseph interpreting Pharaoh's dream; Joseph being made ruler of Egypt; Joseph revealing himself to his brothers; Joseph welcoming his father, Jacob, to Egypt (partially obscured); Jacob blessing Joseph's sons. The Samuel Window on the right reads from bottom to top of both lancets and shows: Samuel presented to God by his mother; Samuel ministering in the Temple; Samuel's call to be a prophet of the Lord; Samuel's prayers routing the Philistines; Saul being anointed; David being anointed; Samuel's home in Ramah; Samuel the prophet and judge (partially obscured). The remaining six windows in the chapel on either side of the central three depict, from left to right: Isaiah, Daniel, Abraham, David, Elijah, and Jeremiah.

The rest of the windows in the church portray the entire life of Christ. The east window tells the story of his Passion, the west window his Resurrection. The eight clerestory windows reflect the story of his life from the Annunciation and the Nativity through his ministry. The seven aisle windows illustrate his prayer taught to the disciples. The cloister, a faithful replica of the cloister at Melrose Abbey, contains in each of its seven bays stained glass medallions of men who have made worthy contributions to the Christian life of the world. Their names are given beneath each of their portraits. These windows are the work of the Detroit Stained Glass Works.

Kirk in the Hills, designed by Wirt Rowland and completed by George D. Mason and Company in 1958, is probably one of the last great structures in America to be built in the classic Gothic tradition. It was inspired by the ancient ruins of the thirteenth-century Melrose Abbey in Scotland, and the Melrose Chapel features one of the stones from the Melrose ruins dated 1246 A.D. The church is cruciform in shape with the baptistry located in the south transept and the Melrose Chapel in the north transept. The exterior of the church features four different grades of Indiana limestone, standard buff, light gray, vomona red, and variegated, used at random to give the exterior of the edifice a striking, colorful appearance. The exterior also features carvings of biblical figures as well as cheerful likenesses of the various artisans who had a hand in building the church.

The interior of the church is dominated by the magnificent stained glass windows. Other features are the Pewabic tile in the narthex and the Melrose Chapel, the fine carvings throughout the church, and the special design of the organ, the unique Trompette-en-Chamade (pipes that project horizontally and are arranged in the shape of a Gothic arch). The trompette is voiced to achieve the effect of the royal trumpeters in the English cathedrals and is the only one of this design in the world. It was designed by the Aeolian-Skinner Company in Boston.

In 1935 Edwin S. George, a successful businessman and investor, established a foundation to build and endow the church. In 1947 he gave Cedarholm, his Tudor-style residence, to the foundation. Now known as Kirk House, the home is connected to the church by the cloister.

75

MARINERS' CHURCH

Address: 170 East Jefferson at Randolph
Architect: Calvin N. Otis, 1849
Window: The Browning Window
Artist: J. and R. Lamb Company, New Jersey, 1959

The rose window in Mariners' Church is a memorial from the Browning family, honoring their mother, Bertie Ann Browning. Replicating a ship's compass, the window is an appropriate tribute inasmuch as the Browning family was associated with shipping on the Great Lakes and owned the Bob-Lo boats and Bob-Lo Island.

In Christian tradition the circular rose window expresses man's sense of the eternal in the universe and in himself. Two of the most popular themes for these windows are Christ the Apocalyptic Judge, and Christ with the Virgin. Sometimes the figurative subject matter is rejected in favor of purely decorative patterns of foliage and bright colors. A good example of the purely decorative is the rose window of Blessed Sacrament Cathedral. The Browning Window illustrated here is unique in that its motif is that of a ship's compass, but still it incorporates many old Christian symbols. The center of the tracery is the ship of the church. In the ship are seen the heads of the Twelve Apostles, including Judas although he was never a popular shipmate. The mast rises upward with the crossbar and reminds one of the cross of Christ with the glow of the rising sun on the outspread sail. The ship rides over the waves of the "waters of life," a symbol of the Church and of each voyager. This symbol was chosen because the first impulse of the apostles was to sail forth around the Mediterranean Sea. Surrounding this central symbol is the formalized mariner's compass, which itself has been used throughout the ages as a Christian symbol because it reflects the great cross of nature formed by the four directions. The compass has four main spokes that radiate vertically and horizontally. Here, these spokes are embellished by the symbols of the Four Evangelists. To the north is the symbol of St. Matthew, a winged figure of a man, emphasizing the human spirit of Christ. To the south is the symbol of St. Mark, a winged lion, representing power and loyal dignity. To the west is the symbol of St. Luke, a winged sacrificial ox that echoes the sacrifice of Zacharias at the opening of St. Luke's Gospel. To the east is the symbol of St. John, an eagle, which exemplifies power and victory and soars to heaven in representation of divine inspiration. Behind the points of the compass is an indication of the mariner's wheel. The circular band symbolizes eternity and is traditionally used around the cross-arms of the cross. This rose compass is composed of pot-metal and painted glass in brilliant colors of red, royal blue, aquamarine, red, pink, and yellow.

All the stained glass windows in the church were designed and made by the J. and R. Lamb Studios of New Jersey after the church was moved from Woodward and Woodbridge to its present location in 1955. They are a veritable lesson in the Old and New Testaments. The altar window, designed by Katherine Lamb Tait, is a particularly fine one with Christ reigning in glory with the saints. Written into the window are the words of the favorite hymn of sailors, "Eternal Father Strong to Save." In the south nave large life-size figures of the New Testament are depicted with their symbols: for example, Bartholomew and three knives, the symbol of his being flayed alive. In the north nave are large figures of the Old Testament. Fortunately all the figures are named which then allows one to enjoy the predellas depicting an event for which the subject is noted. Also in stained glass are the four major archangels, Raphael, Gabriel, Michael, and Uriel.

The architectural style of the church is the so-called Perpendicular Gothic, which flourished between the middle of the fifteenth and sixteenth centuries and which is the very last of the modified Gothic styles. Mariners' Church was the first of a series of gray limestone churches that formed the main body of the Gothic revival work done in Detroit during the next quarter century. The stone was obtained from the quarries at Malden and Trenton and the sandstone for trim and carved ornament was obtained from quarries on Lake Erie. The church was the bequest of Charlotte Ann Taylor and her sister Julia Anderson. Since the will stipulated that sittings in the church should be forever free two stores were designated for the ground floor to provide rental revenue. The Detroit Bank and the United States Post Office were the first tenants. The building was moved 880 feet to its present site in 1955 where initially the Old Indian Council House had stood.

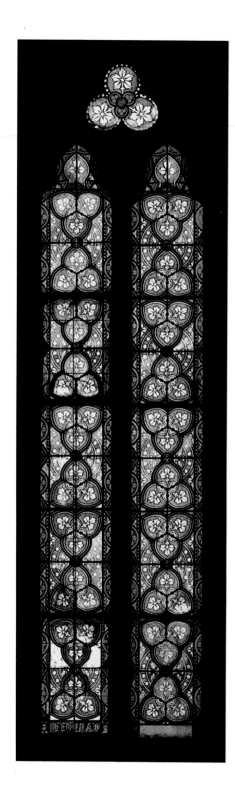

MOST HOLY TRINITY ROMAN CATHOLIC

Address: 1050 Porter at Sixth
Architect: Patrick C. Keeley, 1855
Window: Grisaille Aisle Window
Artist: Ignatius Schott

Grisaille windows, such as the double-lancet window illustrated here, were often installed as temporary measures, to be used only until a church could afford stained glass or until stained glass windows and memorials were donated. Sometimes, as in the case of Most Holy Trinity, the grisaille was not replaced because the congregation preferred the light that this style of window afforded. (For many years the interior of Most Holy Trinity was decorated in dark tones, thus requiring good lighting.)

The grisaille pattern here is a repetitive trefoil. This is in keeping with an often followed tradition that the windows in a church somehow reflect the name of the church, in this case the trefoil is symbolic of the Trinity. It is interesting to note that the trefoil also symbolizes the shamrock, considered the national emblem of Ireland and thus dear to the founding Irish congregation of the church. The leaded trefoil pattern, with ruby pot-metal glass tracing it, has in each foil a stylized three-leaf clover. Each lancet has a narrow border of blue scallops and red triangles in pot-metal glass and silver stain.

All the windows in the church are grisaille, the one exception being the east window. Signed by Ignatius Schott in 1875, the east window is painted enamel glass. It shows Christ as the central figure with the face of God and the dove of the Holy Spirit above, the symbolic three of the Holy Trinity. Below the figure of Christ, the Last Supper is depicted.

Most Holy Trinity parish was established for the large Irish influx of the early 1830s. The Irish left their native land largely because of the potato famine, but also because of political unrest. They began to arrive in Detroit in considerable numbers in 1833. Rev. Martin Kundig under the direction of Bishop Frederick Rèse organized Holy Trinity parish in 1834. They purchased the little wooden church of the First Protestant Society and moved it to what is now Cadillac Square. Before the first service could be held, the cholera epidemic of 1834 struck, and the little church was transformed into a hospital,

the church pews serving as beds. Holy Trinity thus is credited with being Detroit's first hospital.

In 1849 the church building was moved again, this time on rollers to its present location. By 1855 a larger building was needed, and architect Patrick C. Keeley drew up plans, constructing the new church around the walls of the old one. The old church was then demolished in 1856. The exterior of the church is of local red brick. A central frontal tower dominates the simple facade, and there are sloping side aisles. The interior comprises a nave and two side aisles divided by a rhythm of Gothic arches. The rear balcony was added in 1890. The tracker organ built in 1867 by Andreas Moeller is the oldest existing organ built in the State and the oldest still in its original location. It reputedly incorporates parts from the first organ in Michigan, which was brought to the area by Father Gabriel Richard.

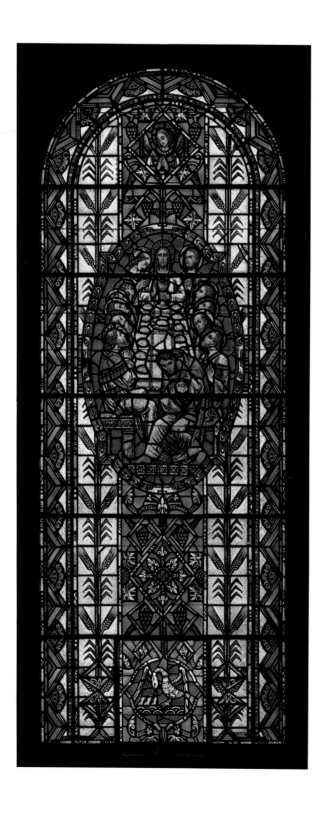

NATIVITY OF OUR LORD CHURCH

Address: 5900 McClellan at Shoemaker
Architects: Vanleyen, Schilling, and Ledugh, 1925
Window: The Last Supper, south aisle
Artist: Conrad Schmidt Studios, Milwaukee, Wisconsin

In paintings of the Last Supper the traitor, Judas Iscariot, is typically shown sitting apart from the other disciples turning away from them, or springing up from the table, as he is shown here, clutching his moneybag containing the thirty pieces of silver. Jesus sits at the head of the table with John at his right hand. The focus of this round-arched window is the large medallion in the center containing precisely this depiction of the Last Supper. The two-dimensional window is executed in medieval style with pot-metal glass, the color predominantly deep blue. Above the central scene is a praying angel, and below it, the pelican piercing its breast to feed its young with its own blood. The legend of the pelican came to symbolize Christ's sacrifice on the Cross. In a sense it also symbolizes the Eucharist, or Lord's Supper, a ceremony instituted by Christ in anticipation of his death and the basis of the Christian Sacrament of Holy Communion. The outer border around the window is executed in geometrical shapes in blue tones with touches of red and silver stain. Between this and the main scene are ribbons of stylized wheat and grapes, the wheat representing the body of Christ and the grapes, Christ's blood. Grapes used with the ears of corn symbolize the wine and bread of Holy Communion.

There are twelve windows in the north and south aisles; all are designed in similar fashion to the one illustrated here, and all are by the Conrad Schmidt Studios of Milwaukee. The central medallions in the windows illustrate the Last Supper (shown here), "Suffer the little children to come unto me" (Matt. 19:13–15), the Good Shepherd, St. Peter, the raising of Lazarus, Christ's miracle at Cana (the changing of water into wine), the Baptism of Christ, the holy family in the carpenter's shop, the boy Christ in the Temple, the presentation in the Temple, the Nativity, and the Annunciation. The north and south transepts contain figures of saints and the Four Evangelists. The sixteen clerestory windows are composed of gold opalescent glass bordered by a red and blue geometrical design. The west rose window is done in geometrical patterns of blue, red, green, and gold pot-metal glass and floods the nave with color in the setting sun.

In 1911 Father Francis Heidenrich was asked by Bishop John S. Foley to start a new parish in Leesville, now the Gratiot-Harper area. The cornerstone of the school was laid in 1912 and the school basement was used for the Church of the Nativity until 1926. The present Renaissance revival church was designed with a facade similar to the basilica church of St. Francis of Assisi in Assisi, Italy. The church is a handsome red-brick structure with a round-arched entrance and a rhythm of arched windows along each side which are faced in stone. An outstanding feature is the campanile capped by a dome on the right of the church. The interior contains a nave and side aisles with marble-faced corinthian columns. Notable is the coffered ceiling. The first mass was celebrated in the new church in 1926, but the church was not completed until 1929.

OUR SHEPHERD LUTHERAN

Address: 2225 East Fourteen Mile Road, Birmingham
Architects: Glen Paulson and Associates, 1966
Window: Detail from the stained glass wall of the church
Artist: Gabriel Loire Studios, Chartres, France.

A continuous wall of dalle-de-verre stained glass windows is a prominent part of this modern church. Dalle-de-verre, also called faceted or scab glass, features large faceted-glass pieces arranged mosaic-style with concrete, or an epoxy material, filling the interstices. The composition of dalle-de-verre produces strong panels and even sturdy walls, a unique feature utilized for the first time in Metropolitan Detroit in the stained glass wall of Our Shepherd Lutheran. The light through the brilliantly colored glass bathes the walls and pews of the church in the strong, primary colors of the windows.

There are a series of seven windows in the wall of the church, each composed of four panels. The detail, illustrated here, represents four of the windows. On the left is the Baptismal Window, featuring a large red anchor, symbol of the seal of the Covenant and the anchor of a faith in God. Next, the window of the Ten Commandments, partially obscured by a large pillar, represents God's Law. The third window signifies the Four Gospels (which contain the story of the life, death, and Resurrection of Christ) represented by the names of the Four Evangelists, Matthew, Mark, Luke, and John. The last window shown here centers on prayer. Folded hands with lines stretching upward symbolize the Christians' confidence and trust in God as he sends his petitions to the golden throne of grace above.

The three other windows in the stained glass wall begin with the bay closest to the lectern. The first depicts the victorious Lamb of God with the banner of the cross, symbolic of "Our Shepherd"; the next window focuses upon the Communion chalice and grapes used to make wine; and the third window, known as the Confirmation Window, represents the Holy Spirit, symbolized by a dove. The Trinity Window in the baptistry off the chancel is also composed of dalle-de-verre glass

furnished by the Blenko Glass Company of Milton, West Virginia, and designed by the Hopfensperger Architectural Art Studio, Midland. The window almost fills the seventy-foot baptistry.

The church is simple in structure without resorting to traditional forms. It is an asymetrical brick building with a lower corner tower and a shed roof leading up to a narrow clerestory. The sweeping slope of the roof flows from the height of the single-story school building to the higher mass desired for the church. The exterior walls are of dark, rough, textured brick, and the roof a gray slate. Indirect light from the clerestory and tower illuminates the unadorned natural brick walls, the clear cypress ceiling and balcony, and the light sculptured oak benches. The simplicity of the chancel focuses all attention to the massive granite altar and the freestanding sixteen-foot teakwood cross. The thirty-six-rank Cassavanti-Freres organ, designed to fit the sloping form of the building, is located in the rear choir balcony. (A thirty-six-rank organ is one composed of thirty-six different sets of pipes.) The exposed pipes add to the beauty and dignity of the rear of the sanctuary. The liturgical vessels were created by Richard Thomas, head of the metal studio at Cranbrook Academy of Art.

SACRED HEART

Address: 1000 Eliot at Rivard
Architect: Peter Dederichs, 1875
Window: Sacred Heart, north nave
Artist: Friedericks and Wolfram, 1899–1911

The window of the Sacred Heart is a two-panel window with rounded arches united by a circle containing the initials IHS, a transliterated abbreviation of the name of Jesus in Greek. The figures contained in the two panels are those of Jesus revealing his Sacred Heart and St. Marguerite Marie Alacoque. Blessed Mary Alacoque, as she is known here, was born in France in 1647 and died there in 1690. She was canonized in 1920. According to the Roman Catholic faith, the command condoning the devotion paid to the Sacred Heart of Jesus was revealed to the French nun through her visions of Christ. Her treatise describing her visions was published in Lyon in 1684. Although private devotion to the Sacred Heart had long existed, public observance spread rapidly thereafter. In 1856 the rite was extended to the universal church by Pope Pius IX.

Above the figures in the window is the large patterned floral and geometrical design that came to be associated with the Detroit Stained Glass Works. These windows were designed by the firm of Friedericks and Wolfram, forerunner of the Detroit Stained Glass Works, in opalescent and painted enamel glass. The colors of the window are predominantly yellow and brown tones, along with lavender, blue, and purple—colors typically associated with the Detroit firm.

The remaining windows in the church are similar in pattern with large figures also surrounded by floral and geometrical designs. The north nave contains the Sacred Heart, discussed above; St. Vincent de Paul with an orphan child; St. Anthony and St. Aloysius; and St. Augustine and St. Dominic. In the south nave are depictions of the Annunciation; a guardian angel with a child; St. John the Evangelist and St. James the Apostle;

and St. Catherine and St. Monica. Two large windows in each nave are purely decorative as are the three west windows.

Sacred Heart Church is an offshoot of Old St. Mary's and was originally a German congregation. It was established at its present location as a mission church in 1875. The church building was designed by a seventeen-year-old parishioner of Old St. Mary's, Peter Dederichs, later one of Detroit's prominent architects. The building has a tall central tower and sloping side aisles, a characteristic of southern German churches. It is built of brick. The interior contains no columns, and the east end is formed into three rounded arches, three being the symbol of the Trinity.

In 1938 Sacred Heart became the home of St. Peter Claver, the first black congregation in Detroit, which also started at Old St. Mary's in 1911. The church was named after a Spanish missionary who went to South America to minister to black slaves in the fifteenth century. The Detroit congregation had maintained its own modest church at Eliot and Beaubien until the parish grew so large that it joined with Sacred Heart, moved into its church, and took its name.

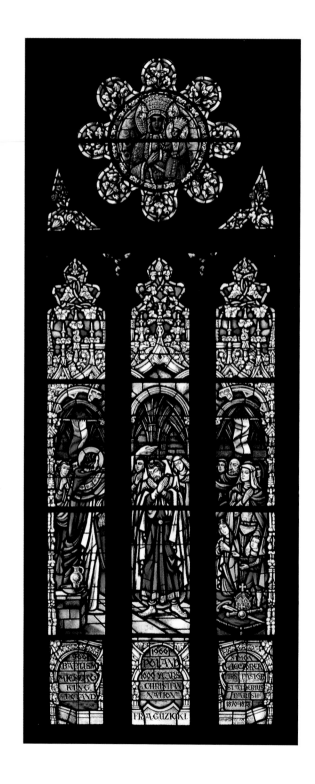

ST. ALBERTUS

Address: 4231 St. Aubin at East Canfield
Architect: Henry Englebert, Detroit, 1884
Window: The Baptism of Miesiekg, King of Poland, A.D. 960, third bay of
*   south wall*
Artist: Thompson Glass Company, Detroit, 1966

This window celebrates Poland's one thousand years as a Christian nation. It also memorializes the first pastor of St. Albertus, Father Simon Wiesczgrek. It is a three-lancet window depicting the baptism of the Polish king. His crown, scepter, and sword are put to one side while a Polish saint baptizes him. A ewer and basin are to the left of the saint, symbols of innocence and purity. Surrounding the king and witnessing his baptism are his wife and two children with other dignitaries. They are dressed in the costume of the period and are standing in what appears to be the nave of a Gothic church. The canopies in the three lancets are architectural and the lancets are united above by a large circle containing the Virgin and Child, both wearing heavy, elaborate crowns that require the diminutive angels on either side to support them. The large circle is surrounded by semicircles depicting the lily, symbol of the Virgin. Although this is a modern window, having been installed in 1966, it is carried out in the manner of the nineteenth-century windows in the church. It is heavily painted with enamel and the life-sized figures are realistic.

Except for seven windows of different colors in geometric patterns installed by the Detroit Stained Glass Works in 1889, the remaining windows in the church are by the Mayer Company of Munich, Germany. The two central chancel windows have figures of St. Henry and St. Boniface. The windows on the sides of the chancel represent the biblical scenes of the offering of Melchizedek, and Christ blessing children. The three transept windows at the north are Moses at the Rock, The Assumption of the Virgin, and Christ the Child; those at the south are The Death of St. Joseph, St. Stanislaus Kostka, and St. Stanislaus Martyr, Bishop of Cracow. In the south nave are windows depicting the washing of Christ's feet at the Last Sup-

per, the Resurrection of Lazarus, and the baptism of the King of Poland. The north nave windows depict the father welcoming home his prodigal son, Lazarus at the table of the rich man, and decorative motifs. In the spandrels are paintings of famous Polish churches.

St. Albertus parish was organized in 1870 for the Polish people who arrived in Detroit in the mid-nineteenth century, and included all Poles living east of Woodward Avenue. Due to the difficulties in finding a correct English equivalent for the name of their Polish-Bohemian patron saint of the church, St. Wojciech, the early pastors and parishioners borrowed the erroneous Latin equivalent Adalbertus, translating it into English as St. Albertus or St. Albert. To this day, one of the Sunday masses is given in Polish.

The brick western-Polish Gothic structure, dedicated in 1885, holds a strong resemblance to the German style of a frontal tower and sloping side aisles because the early Poles in Detroit came from German-occupied Poland. It is an imposing structure dominated by a tower 280 feet high. The interior is treated in medieval style, reflecting the nineteenth-century practice.

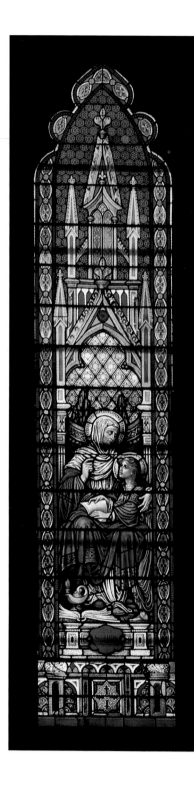

ST. ANNE ROMAN CATHOLIC

Address: 1000 St. Anne at Howard
Architect: Albert E. French, 1886
Window: St. Anne and the Virgin, sanctuary above the altar
Artist: Detroit Stained Glass Works, 1888

This lancet window, one of five in the clerestory of the east end of the church, depicts St. Anne, patroness of the church. She is seated among Gothic architecture with a book open, instructing her child, the Virgin Mary, who is leaning against her knee. St. Anne is clothed in red, symbol of love and martyrdom. Mary is clothed in a mantle of blue, a traditional color for both Christ and the Virgin Mary. A lighted lamp and another open book are at their feet. A grisaille trefoil frames the head of St. Anne and the silver stain Gothic spires behind her are set against deep blue grisaille, blue for heaven and heavenly love. The four other lancets surrounding this central one of St. Anne with the Virgin represent the four patron saints of France, St. Eloi, St. Remi, St. Martin, and St. Denis. The five apse lancets are done in brilliant colors that draw the eye to the sanctuary.

To the north of the chancel, the Chapel of Our Lady of Guadalupe contains a stained glass window with three saints. These are French saints although the chapel itself is dedicated to a Mexican deity, reflecting the predominance of Spanish speaking people in the congregation today. To the south of the sanctuary is the St. Joseph Chapel. Here, again, three saints are depicted in one window. This window bears the signature of the company responsible for the windows in these two chapels and in the nave; it reads: "Bavaria Art Glass Studios, Minpls [Minneapolis], Minn." The same signature is to be found in different lettering on the west window of the north nave above the name of St. Cecile. All of the windows depict saints with their names lettered beneath them. They are large figures in frontal positions, realistically represented in painted enamel.

The two large transept windows are relatively new, having replaced older ones blown out in a storm. The north transept shows Christ preaching and below it a predella with the Last Supper. Below this, on the nave level is a smaller window representing Immaculate Mary. It is signed: "Buffalo Stained Glass Works, Buffalo, New York." In the corner of this transept is the Chapel of the Virgin, containing two windows, each with three saints. The large window in the south transept is the Adoration of the Magi, with Christ entering Jerusalem in the predella. The lower window, again signed "Buffalo Stained Glass Works, Buffalo, New York" depicts the Sacred Heart of Jesus. The corner chapel in this transept is dedicated to the Sacred Heart and has two windows with three saints in each. The large West Rose Window is nonrepresentational. It is of pot-metal glass.

When Cadillac landed in Detroit in July 1701, he immediately began the construction of Fort Pontchartrain du Detroit. Among the first straw-thatched log structures was a small chapel that, tradition asserts, was started on July 26, the feast day of St. Anne, the patron saint adopted by the early French pioneers traveling in the New World. Four churches were successively built on this site (just west of what is now Jefferson Avenue and Griswold) before the disastrous fire of 1805. A Franciscan priest accompanied Cadillac, and that Order ministered to the Detroit parish for almost a century. In 1798 Father Gabriel Richard of the Supulcian Order arrived at St. Anne's, and with good reason he has been termed the "second founder of Detroit." In his thirty-two years at St. Anne's Father Richard wore many hats: priest, patriot, founder of churches and schools, co-founder, with the Reverend John Monteith, of the University of Michigan, member of Congress, and printer. In his sixty-fifth year, 1832, Father Richard died of cholera.

The seventh edifice of St. Anne's was built in 1818 during Father Richard's tenure and was located where the Greyhound Bus Terminal now stands at 130 East Congress. The grisaille windows in the clerestory of the present St. Anne's came from that church. The present structure (the eighth St. Anne's, at Howard and St. Anne streets) is built of brick with two tall frontal towers with spires, following French prototypes rather than English ones. The interior is cruciform in plan and comprises a narthex, nave, two side aisles, transepts, and chancel. Behind the chancel is the chapel, which has recently been redecorated. This chapel contains the altar from the 1818 church and the tomb of Father Richard. The interior contains polychromed images, and the vaulted ceiling is painted heavenly blue and filled with stars.

ST. ANTHONY

Address: 5247 Sheridan
Architect: Donaldson and Meier
Window: St. Boniface, St. Anthony of Padua, and St. Zenobius
Artist: G.T.A. Studios, Innsbruck, Austria

All of the windows in St. Anthony Church except the west window are from Innsbruck, capital of the Tyrol, a province of Austria noted for its glassmaking. These windows, typical of the Renaissance style of the late-nineteenth and early-twentieth centuries, depict large figures heavily painted in rich dark colors. St. Anthony's windows also make liberal use of silver stain and white glass, which admits light into the church and helps accentuate the richness of colors in the painted figures. Each window represents a religious scene in a single round-arched window topped by a circle that contains a figure or a symbol. The three windows illustrated here are of St. Boniface, St. Anthony, and St. Zenobius. The left window depicts the figure of St. Boniface, an eighth-century archbishop of Mainz who established the foundations of Christianity in Germany. (St. Anthony was primarily a German congregation.) St. Boniface is holding his attribute, a book pierced with a sword, which refers to his defense of the Gospel as he met his death blow. The axe at his feet refers to the fact that he felled the sacred oak tree, Thor. The circle above contains a gold crown signifying victory over death and sin, and white roses, symbol of purity. The figure of St. Boniface fills the entire window.

The center window, larger than those on either side, portrays St. Anthony of Padua for whom the church was named. St. Anthony first joined the Order of St. Augustine, but later joined the Franciscans in Assisi where he soon became the favorite disciple and close friend of St. Francis. St. Anthony taught in the renowned universities of Italy and France. He died in 1231 in Padua when only thirty-six-years old and was later canonized as Padua's patron saint. He is shown here in the robes of the Franciscan Order, and the scene depicts his vision of the Christ Child standing on a book, a book being one of St. Anthony's attributes. A handsome stylized design of lilies, also one of St. Anthony's attributes, fills the rounded top of the window. A dramatic landscape of mountains and trees fills the background. In the circle above is the head of a young person surrounded by flames of fire and more stylized lilies, again representing St. Anthony.

The window to the right depicts St. Zenobius, and his large figure fills the window. He was born in Florence of a noble family in the fourth century and was converted to Christianity by one of his tutors. Many legends are told of his ability to restore the dead to life, and for this reason he is frequently portrayed with a small child in his arms, as he is shown here. When he died, a dead tree touched by his body is said to have burst into leaf. Such a tree can be seen in the background of this window. Contained in the circle above is a red crown, symbol of his noble birth, and lilies, symbol of purity. The west window of the church is by the Detroit Stained Glass Works.

The location for St. Anthony Church has an interesting history. It is part of a 347-acre bequest of one Francois Malcher to the diocese of Cincinnati to which Detroit belonged until 1833. Somehow, the deed to the acreage was lost and the diocese's claim to the property became the subject of a legal dispute. Litigations of one kind and another proceeded until it looked as though the diocese would lose everything. In the end the diocese came away with only 96 acres, while the opposition grew wealthy on the lion's share of 251 acres. Bishop Peter Paul Lefevre, the bishop at the time, donated a part of the remaining 96 acres to the families who were to be St. Anthony's parish. He included a bell for the church they would build and one hundred dollars. The bishop also granted the parish permission to use lumber from the surrounding forest land and in 1857 the men of the parish erected a frame church with a seating capacity of three hundred. The original church built in 1857 still stands; it was sold in 1902 and has served since then to house families who live at 5100 and 5110 Field Avenue. The old church could not have been used for such a purpose had it been consecrated, but it had been blessed only.

Some fifty German families formed the nucleus of St. Anthony parish, an offshoot of Old St. Mary's Church, the first German Roman Catholic parish in Detroit. The present church, a red brick, twin-towered neo-Romanesque-style building, was begun in 1901. Over the years, St. Anthony parish came to be well known for its good schools, the grade school begun in 1896, and the high school in 1918. In 1959 a church bulletin announced: "After consulting with pastors of other parishes, Father finds it necessary to raise the tuition in the Grade School as follows: ten dollars for the first child per year, eight dollars for the second child per year, seven dollars for the third child per year, and the fourth child is free." In 1981 the street directly in front of the church was renamed St. Anthony Place by a vote of the Detroit City Council, and in June 1982 this still-active parish celebrated its 125th anniversary.

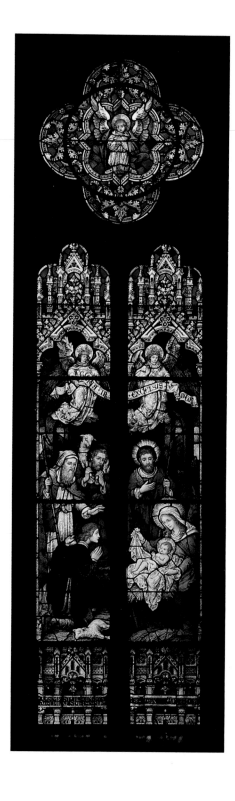

ST. BONIFACE ROMAN CATHOLIC

Address: 2350 Vermont at Michigan
Architect: Scott and Company, 1882–1883
Window: The Nativity, south nave
Artist: Franz Mayer and Company, Munich, Germany, 1909

The Nativity Window is part of a set of windows, designed and executed by the Mayer Studios of Munich, Germany, in 1909, depicting the life of Christ from his birth to his ascension. The story of the Nativity is described in two lancets crowned by a quatrefoil. An angel surrounded by stylized foliage is in the center of the quatrefoil. These windows are typical of the Munich school of the nineteenth century. The figures, modeled on those of the Renaissance, are heavily painted with enamel paint and are rich in deep colors of red, blue, green, and yellow. Light illuminates the realistic figures, which look as though they have been taken from a biblical picture book. The canopies in the space above the figures are a favorite device used by the German Studios to fill large windows. This device was first introduced in the fourteenth century when Gothic cathedrals began to soar and windows became taller and narrower. These architectural canopies resemble the arcading of decorated architecture. Tinted with silver stain these spiry designs also serve the practical purpose of admitting light because the main subject of the window is heavily painted and restricts light. The horizontal bands of canopies unite the groups of lancets and frame the figures that otherwise might appear to float in space. The Nativity, pictured here, shows Joseph and Mary presenting the Christ child to three shepherds, one carrying a lamb. The slain lamb at their feet foretells the future of the Christ child. Above the figures are two angels carrying a banner which reads "Gloria in Excelsis Deo."

The remaining scenes in the Life of Christ windows are grouped together in lancets and crowned by quatrefoil. Besides the Nativity scene, which is signed by the Mayer Studios, the other scenes are: the presentation of the infant Christ in the Temple; the presentation of Christ as a boy in the Temple; Joseph's carpenter's shop; the Baptism; the Sea of Galilee; Christ's Miracle at Cana (the changing of water into wine); the Sermon on the Mount; the transfiguration; "Suffer the little children to come unto me" (Matt. 19:13–15); Christ's entry into Jerusalem; the Last Supper; Gethsemane; the Resurrection; the Ascension; and Pentecost.

St. Boniface Church started as a German parish in 1869 and was the third offshoot of Old St. Mary's in what we know as Greektown. St. Boniface was the archbishop of Mainz in the eighth century and established the foundation for Christianity in Germany. His emblem, a gold book pierced by a sword, refers to his defense of the Gospel as he met the blow of death while confirming baptized converts. This German church honors St. Boniface. Construction of the permanent church building began in 1882 and the result is the church we see today. The building is Gothic revival in style, cruciform in plan, and has a frontal tower and sloping side aisles. The exterior is of red brick with decoration afforded by a light-colored contrasting stone over the windows and doors and on the facade. The interior is a nave and two aisles separated by Gothic arches resting on rows of columns. The walls and ceiling were originally elaborately decorated but now are obscured by paint. The carved wooden altar is a particularly fine one and worthy of note.

ST. CATHERINE AND ST. EDWARD

(Formerly St. Catherine of Siena)
Address: 4151 Seminole at Sylvester
Architect: Unknown, 1919–1930
Window: St. Catherine of Siena Window, west entrance
Artist: Willet Studios, Philadelphia

In the late 1940s the interior of this handsome Renaissance-style church underwent beautification. The plain glass was removed and medieval-style windows were installed. It is unusual to see medieval windows in a Renaissance-style building but in this case it is effective. The pastor at the time, Father John Vismara, worked with Willet in designing a cohesive plan for windows in the entire church. There are fourteen windows in the clerestory; twelve in the aisles; seven in the sanctuary; three in each of the two chapels, and three rose windows. The magnificent triptych in the west wall over the main entrance is illustrated here.

The St. Catherine of Siena Window is one of the finest Willet windows in Detroit. It depicts scenes from the life of the patroness of the church. In the east panel is St. Catherine at prayer at the tomb of St. Agnes. Below this picture is a representation of St. Catherine receiving the stigmata, corresponding to the five wounds in the hands, feet, and side of Christ. Below this is St. Catherine in ecstasy. The top section of the west panel shows St. Catherine visiting the sick in her native city of Siena, in the center she is shown as peacemaker in the wars between the Republic of Siena and Florence, and in the lower portion she receives the last Sacraments. The upper section of the center of the triptych depicts St. Catherine in glory, while in the bottom section of the same panel she is dictating letters to the immense number of people who seek her counsel. The center section shows St. Catherine trying to persuade Pope Gregory XI to return to Rome, his See, from Avignon in France where Pope Clement V had transferred the seat of the Church in 1305. It is thought that St. Catherine was the greatest single influence in bringing the Pope back to Rome in 1378. Note that in this scene the Pope has at his elbow a little imp with horns tugging at his sleeve to persuade him to remain in Avignon, whereas at St. Catherine's elbow there is a little angel tugging at her sleeve assisting her to persuade the Pope to return to Rome. The whole triptych is framed with the heads of angels.

The large rounded windows of this church are now filled with medieval-type glass and the jewellike pieces of pot-metal glass with their intense red, blue, and green colors cast a subdued and reflective mood throughout the church. Each of the fourteen clerestory windows contains one of the stations of the cross, a unique representation in Detroit. In each of the aisle windows is the image and symbol of one of the Twelve Apostles; in the sanctuary a representation of each of the seven Sacraments; and in the two chapels there are scenes from the life of the Virgin and St. Joseph. The pot-metal stained glass in these windows is worthy of note for they are among the finest that Willet has produced. Each piece of glass chosen is rich in color, and each piece of glass is of different shape and of different and irregular thickness to give a better treatment to the light that penetrates through.

St. Catherine of Siena's architecture is a fine example of the Renaissance style, which emphasizes simplicity and elegance in all its lines. The various pictures and symbols in the interior of the church are a virtual lesson in the history of the Roman Catholic Church from its beginnings. Anyone interested in the history of the Roman Catholic faith would do well to start here.

ST. FLORIAN

Address: 2626 Poland, Hamtramck
Architect: Ralph Adams Cram, 1927–1928
Window: The Crucifixion
Artist: Franz Mayer and Company, Munich, Germany

The window of the Crucifixion is one of a set of nine executed by the Mayer Studios of Munich, Germany, for St. Florian from 1934 to 1936. It is interesting to note the change in style from the St. Boniface windows done by the same studios in 1909. The realistic, life-sized figures in the St. Boniface windows are in the Renaissance manner with large areas of painted enameled glass. The St. Florian windows by Mayer demonstrate a rediscovery of the essential character of medieval glass, which prefers a simpler and more austere technique. The figures in The Crucifixion are simplified and stylized, pot-metal glass is used, and the pieces of glass are smaller and jewellike with leading boldly outlining the design. The colors are the deep blue, red, and green used by the medieval craftsman. The crucified Christ is flanked on one side by the Virgin Mary, on the other by John the Baptist. At Christ's feet is Mary Magdalene, symbol of the repentant sinner. A skull, the symbol of death, is at her feet. At the top of the window is a pelican. According to legend, the pelican has the greatest love of all creatures for its offspring, piercing its breast to feed them with its own blood. Based on this legend, the pelican has become a symbol of Christ's sacrifice on the cross because of his love for all mankind. The predellas illustrate the instruments of Christ's Passion: a ladder, scourge, spear, axe, and pincers. The ladder with a reed and sponge crossing it represents the attempt to alleviate Christ's suffering with vinegar mingled with gall.

The altar windows, the nave windows, and the rose window were done by the Kase Company of Philadelphia. The altar windows represent five Polish saints: St. Casimir, St. Stanislaus, St. Hedwig, St. Hyacinth, and St. Florian. The nave windows represent the life and teachings of Christ, and the beautiful rose window centers on the Virgin surrounded by saints.

St. Florian, the Roman soldier saint who is the namesake of the church, was born near Vienna ca. A.D. 280. He was martyred for his faith by being thrown into the river Enns in Upper Austria with a stone tied to his neck, thus his symbol is a millstone. He was first buried near where drowned but his body was later transferred to Rome. In 1184, at the request of King Casimir of Poland, St. Florian's relics were transferred to Crakow. He is credited with saving the city from a devastating fire and thus became known as the patron saint of firefighters. St. Florian is also the patron saint of Poland and Upper Austria. When a group of Polish people first suggested a church in Hamtramck in 1907 it was natural to turn to a saint identified with their homeland. A small church was built in 1908 on the present site and was replaced in 1928 by the much larger modified English Gothic church we see today.

ST. JOHN'S ARMENIAN

Address: 22001 Northwestern Highway, Southfield
Architect: Suren Pilafian, 1968
Window: Detail from a window in the enclosing masonry walls
Artist: Gabriel Loire Studios, Chartres, France

The octagonal shape of St. John's Armenian Church was inspired by several round churches built in Armenia. Each of the eight enclosing masonry walls include pairs of tall, faceted windows of dalle-de-verre glass. The dalle-de-verre technique, akin to mosaic, lends itself to abstract and highly stylized designs evidenced in the window illustrated here. Typically Armenian ornamental motifs such as crosses, birds, fish, grain stalks, and flowers are used here as well as in all sixteen windows of the enclosing church walls. The location of the windows was planned to produce a dramatic effect and to enhance the impact of the interior design. A walk around the nave provides you with changing glimpses of the windows and different effects. If you stand in the center of the nave all the windows are hidden from sight, but a warm multicolored light is reflected on the masonry walls.

There are sixteen additional dalle-de-verre windows radiating from the central disc at the top of the domed ceiling. They portray saints important to the Armenian church—thirteen apostles and three Armenian saints. Saint Gregory the Illuminator, evangelist of the Armenians and the patron saint of Armenian churches, is placed in the window just above the altar. He is flanked on either side by the two saints considered the founders of Armenian literature—St. Sahag, translator of the Bible into Armenian, and St. Mesrob, the originator of the Armenian alphabet.

St. John's Church reflects the achievements of Armenian builders during the millennium preceding the fourteenth century, a time that saw five thousand Christian churches built in Armenia. The form, material, and design of this church recall the basic designs, ideas, elements, and philosophy of that millennium. The churches in Armenia used stone for all parts of the structure because the mountainous character of the topography made stone the most readily available permanent building material. The buff variegated Indiana limestone used on St. John's is reminiscent of that custom. The octagonal shape of the building, as already noted, developed from round churches in Armenia, and a crowning central dome is a typical feature of Armenian churches. St. John's dome is covered with a serrated, conical, jewellike peaked roof, sheathed with pure gold. (It may be noted that the serrated roof was used in Armenia nine hundred years before it became popular in the modern buildings of today.) St. John's golden dome, shooting skyward for ninety feet, a landmark in Detroit, commands attention from the roadways and expressways that surround it. The architectural design of the church, also reflecting the designs of churches in Armenia, includes a system of crossing semicircular arches to support the serrated conical gold-covered dome, blind arches, stone framed doors and windows, ornamental stone carvings, and an entrance portico with a belfry.

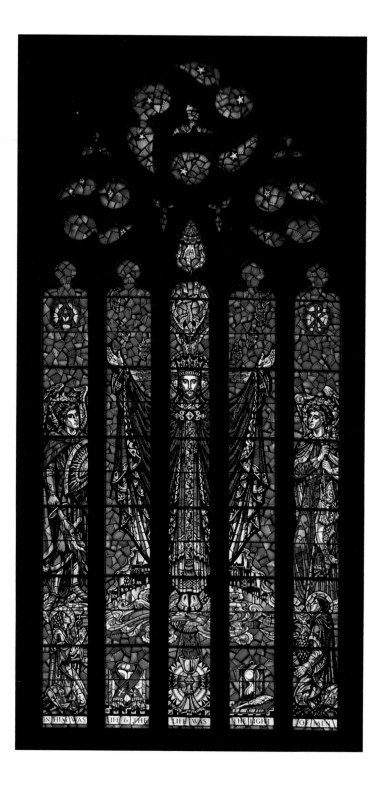

ST. JOHN'S EPISCOPAL

Address: 50 East Fisher Freeway (I-75) at Woodward
Architects: Albert Jordan and James Anderson, 1861
Window: The Triumphant Christ, west window
Artist: J. Wippell and Company, Ltd., Exeter, England, 1963

For more than a hundred years the great west window of St. John's Church waited to receive a fitting subject in stained glass. In 1963 this window was installed in memory of Rev. Canon Irwin Chester Johnson, a rector of St. John's, and of organist and choirmaster John Leigh Edwards, who had served the congregation for forty years. A five-lancet window with bold tracery above, it is made entirely of hand-blown pot-metal glass from England, Germany, and France. The window, executed in the mosaic style and with the decorative detachment of the Middle Ages, displays a rich blue background with a variety of colors shown in the garments of the saints, but all subordinated to the vivid red of Christ's robes. The dominant figure is Christ displaying the stigmata, his feet separately fastened, as in the Byzantine fashion, and his head crowned to signify his kingship. Above the figure of Christ are the dove of the Holy Spirit and the hand of God, completing the Trinity. They are surrounded by seven tongues of flame, symbolizing the seven gifts of the Spirit. The tracery above contains abstract patterns in tones of blue with a gold star in the center of each opening. Behind Christ at his feet is the City of Jerusalem and below this, flowing into the chalice, is his blood, symbolic of his sacrifice. The central figure in the left lancet is that of St. Michael holding a flaming sword. St. Michael is recognized as the leader of all spiritual forces against the powers of darkness. He also symbolizes the discipleship of Christ's earthly priests. Directly above appear the alpha and the omega, the first and last letters of the Greek alphabet, signifying that Christ is the beginning and the end of all things. In the lower portion of the lancet, music is symbolized by the figure of St. Cecelia with a harp. She is regarded as the patroness of church music, and St. John's Church has long been noted for its fine music. St. Raphael, the archangel and guardian of all humanity, is the central figure in the right-hand lancet. St. Raphael holds a fish, ancient symbol of Christianity. Above has been placed the Chi Rho, a monogram of the first two letters, X and P, of the Greek word for Christ. Below St. Raphael is the figure of the patron saint of the church, St. John the Evangelist, symbolized by the eagle. The open book with crossed stole, symbolic of the priesthood, is in the lower panel to the left of the chalice. The closed book and hour glass, depicting the passage of time, is in the lower panel to the right of the chalice.

The ten nave windows are Annunciation and the Flight Into Egypt (1953) by the Lamb Studios; Presentation of Christ in the Temple (1917) and Epiphany (1913) by Gorham; The Young Christ by Tiffany Studios (1897); Christ and Mary of Bethany (1880); St. Agnes (1882) and The Good Shepherd (1898) by Tiffany Studios; and The Marriage Feast at Cana (1953) and The Fisher of Men (1954) also by the Lamb Studios. The east window, Christ Blessing Little Children, by the Detroit Stained Glass Works, is a memorial to a child. The north apse contains the four prophets Isaiah, Jeremiah, Ezekiel, and Daniel. In the pinnacle of the window, Moses holds the Tables of the Law. The south apse windows contain the Four Evangelists, Matthew, Mark, Luke, and John. In the pinnacle of this window appears the figure of St. Paul holding the sword of the Spirit. Except for the three Tiffany windows in opalescent glass, the windows are of large, painted figures typical of the late-nineteenth century.

The cornerstone of St. John's Chapel was laid in April 1859 and the congregation assembled there until the present church was built in 1861. The original chapel remains a part of the church buildings and is still in use. The east window of the chapel, installed in 1919, features St. John pointing to the Gospel. The chapel is similar to the chapel at Elmwood Cemetery, also by Albert Jordan. St. John's Church is Victorian Gothic in style and built of native limestone with sandstone trim. Caenstone is featured in the entrance archway to the nave, the chancel screen, the pulpit, and the altar. The reredos contains a carved copy in Vermont marble of Leonardo da Vinci's painting, *The Last Supper*. The gargoyles which adorn the exterior of the church were made by Walter Schweikart, a stone mason in Detroit highly regarded in his craft. When Woodward Avenue was widened in 1936 the church tower was razed, the church rolled back sixty feet, and the tower rebuilt. Wirt C. Rowland, best known for his decorative design of Detroit's Guardian Building, supervised the task of moving and reconstructing St. John's.

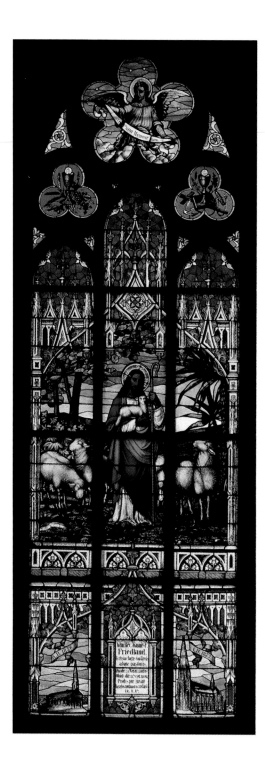

ST. JOSEPH ROMAN CATHOLIC

Address: 1828 Jay Street at Orleans
Architect: Francis J. Himpler, 1873
Window: The Good Shepherd, north aisle

The window of The Good Shepherd is a fitting memorial for the Reverend J. F. Friedland under whose direction St. Joseph and its parish came to full flowering. The Good Shepherd, adapted from the Roman sculpture of a shepherd boy and his lamb, is one of the oldest Christian symbols. In the catacombs of Rome there is a Good Shepherd picture painted in the fourth century A.D., probably just before Emperor Constantine officially recognized Christianity. The figure of Christ represented in this window is typical in Detroit churches of this period, as Victorian Gothic stylistically favored the Renaissance figures rather than the stylized ones of the medieval Gothic period. Renaissance realism tended to become sentimental in the nineteenth century, and we see here Christ as a human being tenderly tending his flock. The Good Shepherd symbol is still a favorite one today and can be found in almost every church denomination in Detroit.

This window uses a combination of pot-metal glass (as seen in the clouds) and painted enamel glass, which is predominant. Windows of three lancets unified by tracery, such as this one, are common in Gothic revival churches, and the style is based on inventions of the fourteenth century. Note too the canopies and architecture filling the top of the window, a favorite design for tall windows for they admirably fill in space. Below the Good Shepherd scene is a memorial to Father Friedland with both the old and the present St. Joseph churches shown in the lower panels. This window was probably made by the firm of Friedericks and Staffin, for its style and its colors are similar to the rose window next to it. We know the latter window, depicting Christ among saints, was given by the Friedericks family and made by their firm.

The stained glass in St. Joseph is a combination of imported and local artistry. The five tall slender windows in the chancel behind the high altar were imported from Munich when the church was built but probably were not made by the Mayer Studios, a favorite in Detroit among the Munich glassmakers. These five windows show the fourteenth-century device for filling tall windows known as "band" windows. A scene in colored glass is depicted, in this case Christ and St. Peter and four saints, and the space above and below the scene is filled with grisaille (in this case, some colored glass has been added). The Death of St. Joseph Window in the south nave was imported from Innsbruck, Austria. The subject is one not usually depicted.

Much of the glass in St. Joseph was made by the Detroit firm of Friedericks and Staffin, the forerunner of the Detroit Stained Glass Works which operated in Detroit until 1970. The rose window above the baptistry is one of theirs and more than likely so is the window of the Holy Family flanked by St. John the Baptist and St. John the Evangelist. The ten grisaille windows of the church are fine examples from this firm.

St. Joseph began as a mission church of Old St. Mary's and therefore served a mostly German population. It has served the near-downtown community for more than a hundred years. Between 1870 and 1873 the present church replaced the simple frame building of the original parish. The church is built of Trenton limestone, the last of the twenty-five year cycle of native limestone churches in Gothic revival style in Detroit. The church is closely modeled on the "hallen-kirchen" (hall churches) of southern Germany, the birthplace of the architect, F. G. Himpler. The ornate details, such as the high altar, are noteworthy in that they are entirely carved from wood. Some wood carvings were imported from Germany, but a parishioner, Anthony Osebold, also made some of them. With its rebuilt tracker organ displaying the original detail work on the pipes and its bells, St. Joseph is a fine example of Victorian Gothic revival.

ST. MARY'S ROMAN CATHOLIC

Address: 646 Monroe at St. Antoine
Architect: Peter Dederichs, 1884
Windows: Decorative windows, north transept
Artists: Friedericks and Staffin, 1885

The north transept of Old St. Mary's contains a number of decorative windows in colored glass, emphasizing the quatrefoil, a design of four leaves. The number four is suggestive of the Four Evangelists. The center circle, or rose window, with a quatrefoil in its center is surrounded by eight circles containing quatrefoil designs. Eight is the number symbol of the Resurrection as it was on the eighth day after Christ's entry into Jerusalem that he rose from the grave. Five small quatrefoils form an arch over the rose window, five for the five wounds of Christ. At each end of the arch there is a double lancet window crowned by a large quatrefoil. Between these latter windows is a round-arched window containing the figure of St. Aloysius holding a cross, symbol of Christ, and a rosary, a form of devotion to the Virgin Mary. St. Aloysius (1568–1591) was a member of the Gonzaga family, a noble family that ruled Mantua Italy from 1308 to 1708. St. Aloysius renounced his position of privilege, entered the church in 1587, and gave his life for the sick during a plague. He was canonized in 1726 and is the patron saint of students. The illustrated windows are of rolled cathedral glass, as are all the windows in the church, and were made by the firm of Friedericks and Staffin in 1885 at a cost of $3,076.45.

St. Mary's Parish was founded in 1840 by Father Martin Kundig, a German Swiss, to accommodate the spiritual needs of the German-speaking Catholics of Detroit. It is the third oldest Catholic parish in the city, preceeded by St. Anne's (French) and Most Holy Trinity (Irish). In 1840 Father Kundig was authorized by Bishop Peter Paul LeFevre to solicit funds for the building of St. Mary's Church. His initial effort raised two dollars and fifty cents. Early in 1841 Antoine and Monica Beaubien sold to Bishop LeFevre, for one dollar, their land at St. Antoine and Croghan Street (now Monroe) to be used for the St. Mary's parish building.

The present church, which replaced the former one in 1884, was designed by Peter Dederichs, a member of St. Mary's parish who was born in Detroit of German parents. He designed the church when he was twenty-eight years old. His architectural plans borrowed elements from the Pisan Romanesque and the Venetian Renaissance and fused them into an original composite design. The church is built of red brick with a basilica style interior. A distinctive feature is the handsome large columns of solid polished granite which were executed originally for a public building in Lansing. When they were found to be the wrong size they were left on the docks in Buffalo. Peter Dederichs heard about them, purchased them for $4,625 and altered his plans for St. Mary's so that they would fit. The church contains three grottos; the baptistry with St. John baptizing Jesus as the Holy Spirit hovers over the Son of God; a replica of the Shrine of Our Lady of Lourdes; and The Agony in the Garden of Gethsemane. These were built personally by the pastor at that time, Rev. Joseph Wuest (1907–1929).

In 1868 the congregation built a school across the street from the church. This building is no longer used as a school. It is still in good condition and the lower floors are used for diverse projects. It is currently under restoration.

ST. PAUL'S CHURCH

Address: 157 Lakeshore Road, Grosse Pointe Farms
Architect: H. J. Rill, 1898
Window: St. Paul Preaching in Athens, south transept
Artist: Franz Mayer and Company, Munich, Germany, 1924

Two unusually large five-lancet windows fill the north and south transepts of St. Paul's Church. The south transept window illustrated here depicts the scene described in the New Testament book Acts of the Apostles in which St. Paul preaches to the Greeks who were curious about the "new religion." Because St. Paul spoke of the resurrection of the dead, the Greeks lost interest, and Paul left Athens and went on to Corinth. This window is mostly enameled glass painted in the fashion prevalent in the early twentieth century. The tracery, leading, and mullions are delicate and serve little purpose in delineating the figures or setting a frame for the picture. St. Paul, with arm raised in exhortation, gowned in a deep purple robe, stands on the steps of a historically correct Doric building situated in the marketplace. On the acropolis in the background is seen the Parthenon, greatest of pagan temples. Among the people gathered to listen to Paul are Greeks, an Oriental potentate, and a Roman magistrate crowned with a laurel wreath, each evidenced by his costume and reflecting the cosmopolitan atmosphere of Athens then as it is today. The scene is realistic from the figure of St. Paul to the note-taking Greeks and the contemplative philosopher. Symbols of pagan and Christian beliefs are represented in the cypress trees (symbol of death), the doves (symbol of purity and peace), and the orange and lemon bearing trees (symbols of purity, chastity, generosity, and fidelity in love). The colors are purple, green, and yellow with the predominant colors being those of the blue sky and sepia Greek buildings. The fleur-de-lis in stained glass borders the window and is replicated in gold leaf on the walls of the apse, an appropriate emblem for a community that was mainly French.

The north transept window is similar in size and execution and depicts the scene of the Nativity. Through the archways in this large painted window are seen the buildings representing the three great religions of the Western world: an Islamic mosque, a Jewish synagogue, and a Christian church. This window is by the Franz Mayer Studios as are the two medallion windows in the sanctuary depicting the Virgin and Child and St. Peter with the keys of the Kingdom. The Great Rose Window in the west facade is the work of Fredericks and Wolfram Art Glass Company of Detroit and was installed in February, 1900. The central medallion depicts St. Paul with a sword, the symbol of the Spirit. The decorative floral and geometric designs of the rose window in pastel colors of pink, green, yellow, red and rose are repeated in the nave windows, also by Friedericks and Wolfram and installed in 1900. Near the top of each of the eight nave windows are medallions that carry a theme that is related to the opposite medallion across the nave. Starting from the front of the nave, the first pair of medallions depict the pope's tiara and the bishop's mitre, symbols of the authority of the Church. The next pair depict Peter's barque and Noah's ark, symbolic of the Church. The third pair portray the instruments of the Passion: hammer, nails, pillar, and whip. The fourth set, the crown and cross, the anchor and the heart are symbolic of the Resurrection and the theological virtues of faith, hope, and love. The windows around the altar were made and installed by the Munich Studios of Chicago in 1924. From left to right they depict the Annunciation, the Nativity, the Crucifixion, the Resurrection, and the Ascension.

An assistant of Father Gabriel Richard, Father Francis Badin, built the first St. Paul's Church in Grosse Pointe in 1825, a small log chapel on the Reno (Renaud) farm on Lake St. Clair just beyond the present Vernier Road. Earlier than that, on the same site, there was a large crucifix, twenty feet high, where early settlers gathered on Sundays to pray. Pierre Provencal also opened his home on his large farm for Sunday services. In 1848 clear title to the present property was obtained. François J. Fresare, who spoke only French, thought he had sold to the church four arpents (an old French land measure often less than an acre) while in fact he had sold four square acres to the church. Disgruntled, he did not give clear title to the property until he received from the church a strip of land sixty-four feet deep running across the back of the property. A frame building was constructed on the church land. In 1898 the present church was built on the same site. It is a red brick and fieldstone building with imposing towers designed in the French Gothic revival style. The main altar, executed in Italy of Carrara marble and onyx was installed in 1910, a replacement for the stone altar which had been in the early St. Paul's. In 1924 the side altars were commissioned to match the high altar. The items in the church today that date to its origins include the pews, rose window, nave windows, baptismal font, and stations of the cross.

ST. PETER'S EPISCOPAL

Address: 1950 Trumbull at Michigan
Architects: Harley and Ellington, Detroit, 1929
Window: Te Deum Window
Artist: James Hogan, Whitefriars Studios, London, England, 1930

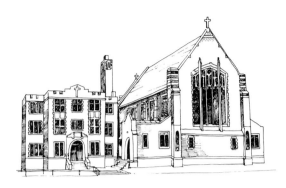

The chancel treatment of St. Peter's is English, characterized by a square sanctuary with a perpendicular traceried window. In 1930 A. A. Buck commissioned a stained glass window for the chancel from James Hogan, a distinguished English glass artist and head of Whitefriars Studios, London. (Hogan also designed the magnificent windows for the churches of St. Thomas and Heavenly Rest on Fifth Avenue in New York City.) The resulting Te Deum Window of five lancets, shown here, is one of the finest stained glass windows in Detroit and illustrates the ancient hymn of unknown origin "Te Deum Laudamas." Whitefriars Studios closed in 1980 but the records, held by the Victoria and Albert Museum in London, reveal that for the St. Peter's window Hogan chose the most expensive and splendid blue and red glass. Three of the completed panels arrived from England prior to World War II, but the remaining two had to wait out the war before reaching Detroit. The window commissioned in 1930 was finally paid for in 1946. It is composed in medieval fashion: two-dimensional, small mosaiclike pieces of pot-metal and Norman slab glass, and the figures are stylized representations in simple lines and little detail. The center lancet is devoted to a bearded Christ in majesty, holding a book with the alpha and omega, Greek alphabet symbols for the beginning and the end. The predominant colors are yellow and gold, a dramatic contrast to the rich reds and blues of the other four lancets. Four archangels in red flank Christ. From left to right they are: St. Uriel holding the sun, a symbol taken from Milton, who in *Paradise Lost* makes Uriel the regent of the sun beguiled by Satan; St. Michael with spear and shield, messenger of divine judgment and leader of all spiritual forces against the powers of darkness; St. Gabriel with a lily, messenger of divine mercy and of good news, was the archangel of the Annunciation who carried a lily and revealed to Mary that she would be the mother of Christ; and St. Raphael with fish and pilgrim's staff, symbols from the Book of Tobit (part of the Apocrypha). Below the archangels are (left to right): the four apostles Peter, Paul, John, and James; John the Baptist with Isaiah and Daniel; the martyrs St. Stephen, St. Margaret of Antioch, and St. Agnes; and St. Augustine, St. Boniface, St. Polycarp, and St. Francis of Assisi. In the predella below Christ is the scene of his crucifixion. The two predellas on the left contain a ship with Jesus and his disciples, symbolic of the Church, and the Madonna and Child. The two predellas on the right contain the Resurrection and the Holy Church with words from the ancient hymn, "The Holy Church throughout the World." In the chapel the Maybury memorial windows, in Renaissance style from the 1870s and 1880s, offer an interesting contrast to the medieval style of the chancel window.

St. Peter's parish was organized in 1857, the fourth Episcopal parish in Detroit and an offshoot of St. Paul's Episcopal Church. Corktown, where St. Peter's is located, was then a suburb of Detroit. Most of the members of St. Peter's came from County Cork, Ireland. Their first church was of wood in carpenter Gothic design. By 1928 the old church was dilapidated and it was condemned. In 1929 the present church, designed by Harley and Ellington, was begun in the style of the then current neo-Gothic churches of the Franciscans and Dominicans. To date the church has not been completed. Because of the lack of funds the rose brick walls have not been plastered and the wood sheathing for the ceiling has not been installed. However, by contemporary standards, exposed internal supports and works have value and are considered aesthetically pleasing. Furnishings of the original St. Peter's have been incorporated in the present building.

ST. STANISLAUS ROMAN CATHOLIC

Address: 5818 Dubois at Medbury
Architect: Harry J. Rill, Detroit, 1911
Window: The Passion of Christ, south transept

The south transept rose window, illustrated here, depicts the Passion of Christ. The window consists of eight large petals with the half figure of the suffering Christ crowned with thorns in the center. Under the figure of Christ the inscription "Catholic Order of Foresters St. Stanislaus, Court # 1202" names a fraternal order founded in 1903. The eight petals symbolize the Resurrection, for it was on the eighth day after his entry into Jerusalem that Christ rose from the grave. Portrayed at the top of each petal is one of the instruments of Christ's Passion (clockwise from bottom right): the column to which he was tied and scourged; the crown of thorns; the cross and reed, mock symbols of power; the whip; a ladder leaning against a cross; hammer and nails; the initials IHS, a transliteration of the first three letters of the name of Jesus in Greek, with the crown of thorns, shroud, and cross; and the initials IHS alone. (The last events of Christ's earthly life, from his entry into Jerusalem to his burial, are collectively called the Passion.) Between the tips of the petals there are small clusters of flowers. The rose window consists almost entirely of yellow-brown opalescent glass, with the Passion symbols composed of green and sepia. This window, and its counterpart in the north transept, were probably executed by a local glass studio.

The remaining windows in the church are probably European and are richly painted in the Renaissance style. Around the apse are windows depicting the Light of the World, an angel and monk, the Virgin Mary, and St. Joseph with a flowering rod. The windows in the nave portray Christ and the rich young ruler, St. Peter receiving the keys of the kingdom, Gethsemane, the Ascension, Mary Queen of Heaven, Christ and Mary, Christ distributing food to the poor, the Madonna, the Annunciation, the Holy Family in the carpenter's shop, Christ in the Temple, and "Suffer the little children to come unto me" (Matt. 19:13–15). The north transept window complements the rose in the south transept. The inscription, "L.B.C.A. St. Stanislaus, Branch 807," remembers the Ladies Benevolent Catholic Association, founded in 1902.

St. Stanislaus, bishop and martyr, was born at Cracow, Poland, in 1030. He was made canon of Cracow and later became its bishop. As bishop, he issued frequent warnings concerning the king's corrupt morals but to no avail. Finally, he excommunicated the king in 1079. The furious monarch ordered Stanislaus put to death, and when his soldiers were unable to carry out his orders because of divine intervention, King Boleslaus himself beheaded Stanislaus.

The Parish of St. Stanislaus was founded in 1898 when Canfield Avenue parishioners living at a distance from Polish churches decided to establish their own church and school. The church committee purchased Beth El Lutheran Church at the corner of Medbury and Dubois for sixteen thousand dollars. In 1903 a school was built next door to the church for the Polish children in the neighborhood. By 1911 the old church had become inadequate for the parish and construction of the present St. Stanislaus church began. The twin-towered yellow brick church is Baroque in style. The facade is in three sections: a two-tiered, columned and pedimented, center portion flanked by two towers that are each topped by three open stages. The interior is reminiscent of European Baroque. The nave is dominated by large round arches and the ceiling and walls are decorated with murals. Corinthian columns in marble frame the elaborate altar and significant statuary is placed about the church.

SWEETEST HEART OF MARY

Address: 4440 Russell at Canfield
Architect: Spier and Rohns, 1893
Window: Holy Family of Nazareth, south transept
Artist: Detroit Stained Glass Works

The sixty-by-thirty-foot south transept window illustrated here depicts the Holy Family at work outside Joseph's carpenter shop. (The window is partially obscured by a hanging lamp and an altar.) Mary is weaving and the child Jesus carries a small cross, symbolic of what the future holds for him. Joseph is glancing at his wife with a sense of foreboding. A dovecote fastened to the wall with doves perching on it foreshadows Jesus' baptism when he saw the Holy Spirit descend as a dove. It is a domestic scene with a cock peacefully pecking the ground for food. Because its crow signals the morning, the cock is used as an emblem of watchfulness and vigilance. There is also a lamb, symbolic of the shepherd and his flock and also of sacrifice. The ax is prominently displayed, an attribute of Joseph and a reference to his trade. The scene resembles a large Renaissance painting with its use of opalescent glass and enamel on glass. The handsome landscape background and life-size, realistic figures add to this effect. The tracery of this window is simplified into three large circles filled with stylized floral ornamentation. The major theme of this floral decoration is the fleur-de-lis, an emblem of royalty given to the Virgin Mary as Queen of Heaven. The side lancets also are filled with elegantly stylized floral designs. The similarly styled north transept window, also sixty by thirty feet, represents the charity of St. Vincent de Paul. These transept windows cost twenty-five hundred dollars each, a considerable sum of money in 1893.

The eight nave windows, four on each side, represent the Good Shepherd and Immaculate Conception; our Lady of Mount Carmel; Christ with the children; St. Agnes with her attribute the lamb, symbol of purity; St. Michael and the dragon; St. Bernadette of Lourdes; St. Dominic and our Lady of the Rosary; and St. Laurence the Martyr. The window depicting the story of the Good Shepherd and Immaculate Conception is the Kolasinski Memorial Window.

All the windows in the church were executed by the Detroit Stained Glass Works. These windows glow with red, orange, blue, and gold hues in various designs and patterns in addition to presenting a biblical or religious scene. The pictorial center of each window is important but the stylized floral decoration and ornamentation around each window in pot metal and silver stain must also be noted for their excellence of design. According to newspaper accounts of the day, the windows won one of the main prizes at the Columbian Exposition of 1893 in Chicago. It is interesting to note that the uppermost part of each window has a large circular design consisting of a cut-out pattern that is a glass rendition of the traditional Polish Eastertide custom of "wycinanki," that is, paper cutouts.

Sweetest Heart of Mary was originally a Polish national church outside the auspices of the Roman Catholic diocese. It was organized in 1888 by a former assistant at St. Albertus, the Reverend D. H. Kolasinski, and a group of his followers from that parish after a dispute with church authorities. The present twin-spired red brick structure is the second church used by the congregation and the largest Roman Catholic church in Detroit. The spires and facade are the focal point of the church. The highly ornamental facade is of Berea stone and blocks. The front has an elaborate main entrance flanked by two side entrances of lesser proportions. Terra-cotta ornamentation is freely used on the church exterior of stock and pressed red brick. The Gothic style of northern Europe never completely lost its hold on Detroit church builders, and its influence can be seen in this church. The interior displays clustered stone piers and ribbed vaults simulated in wood and plaster. The surface of the columns is scagliola, a plaster imitation of ornamental marble. The parish reconciled with church authorities in 1897 and entered a period of growth and prosperity, but it did not become part of the Roman Catholic diocese until after World War II.

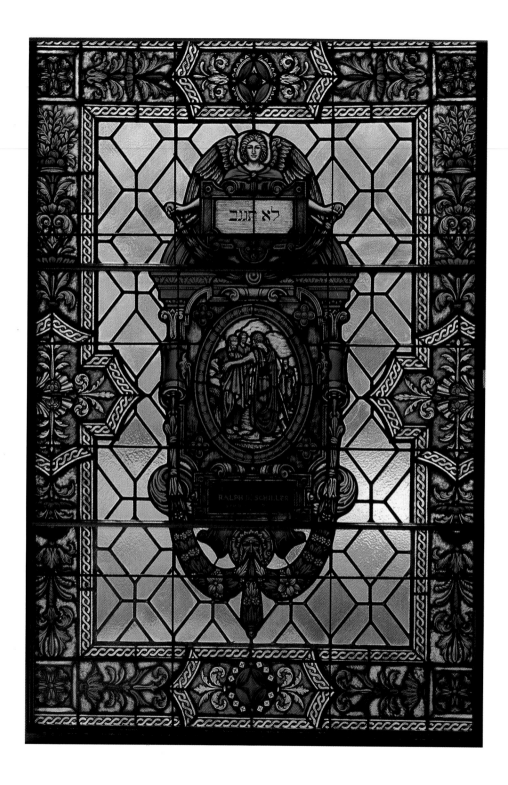

TEMPLE BETH EL

Address: 7400 Telegraph at Fourteen Mile Road, Birmingham
Architect: Minouru Yamasaki, 1973
Window: Thou Shalt Not Steal, sanctuary foyer
Artist: Hinicki and Smith, New York

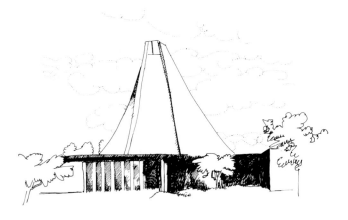

Each of the stained glass windows in the foyer of the Helen DeRoy Sanctuary depicts one of the Ten Commandments issued by God on Mt. Sinai. These windows were installed in the former Temple Beth El at Woodward and Gladstone in two stages—four in 1921, and the remaining six in 1922. The designers copied the style of the painted windows by Thomas Giovanni of Udine in the Certosa Chapel in Florence, Italy. The window illustrated here is the eighth commandment, Thou Shalt Not Steal. The symbolism of this medallion is somewhat obscure. According to the staff at Temple Beth El it was first thought that the window depicted an episode in Genesis where Benjamin was accused of stealing a cup from Joseph's court. On further investigation, however, it was agreed that the incident, which occurs in the desert, and which represents stealing, is the moment in which Korach tries to wrest the reigns of leadership from Moses and is swallowed up by the barren ground of the desert. All ten windows are similar in design and are executed in painted enamel in colors of dark blue, green, red, and gold. Each is bordered by a wide stylized floral design in colors of white and gold with touches of red. The border is then edged by lightly tinted stained glass with a leaded chain link design. The medallion, in the center of a large shield, bears a symbolic rendering of one of the Commandments. The windows are placed in the order in which they were removed from the temple on Woodward and Gladstone rather than in the order of the Ten Commandments. Beginning with the left window facing the door to the sanctuary and proceeding clockwise, the Ten Commandments are: Remember the Sabbath Day (the fourth commandment), Thou Shalt Not Take the Lord's Name in Vain (the second), Thou Shalt Not Covet (the tenth), Thou Shalt Not Commit Adultery (the seventh), Thou Shalt Not Commit Murder (the sixth), Thou Shalt Not Steal (the eighth), Thou Shalt Not Bear False Witness (the ninth), I Am the Lord Thy God (the first), Thou Shalt Not Make Any Graven Image (the third), and Honour Thy Father and Mother (the fifth).

Temple Beth El, Michigan's first Jewish congregation, was founded in 1850. It was organized by twelve German Jews in the home of Mr. and Mrs. Isaac Cozens on Congress and St. Antoine streets. The original congregation was orthodox in its ritual and observance. (In 1862 the congregants adopted a new constitution, paving the way for the Reform Judaism practiced by the congregation today.) The temple on Woodward Avenue and Eliot Street, occupied between 1903 and 1922, was the first place of worship built by the congregation. Albert Kahn, the architect, was a member of the congregation. Except for the fact that it had Ionic columns instead of Corinthian columns on its entrance porch, the temple was a small replica of the Pantheon in Rome. Now it is the home of the Bonstelle Theatre of Wayne State University. Thirteen medallion windows removed from the original temple are set in the glass walls of the passageway joining the administrative building to the foyer of the sanctuary in the present building. The glass in the thirteen medallions is opalescent and the design in each is a floral wreath with the memorial name in the center. In 1922 another temple was built at Woodward and Gladstone. Albert Kahn was also the architect for this classical Greek-style temple. The Ten Commandment windows from this second building were removed by sculptor Gordon Hipp in 1973, altered, and set in the glass walls of the foyer to the new Helen DeRoy Sanctuary. (Sculptor Hipp's works can be seen in the doors to the Administrative Building. They are beveled prism glass and commemorate the three partiachs, Abraham, Isaac, and Jacob.)

Architect Minouru Yamasaki (1912–1985) designed the present Temple Beth El in 1973. The complex consists of the sanctuary itself, an administrative building, a school, and meeting halls for the congregation. Both symbolically and in actuality the sanctuary resembles a great tent. Four huge columns support twin ridge beams between which there is a skylight. Suspended between the ridge beams are steel roof cables that support the lead-coated copper roofing. In the interior stands a tall bronze Torah ark designed by the sculptor Bernard Rosenthal. The walls of the Sanctuary are clear glass.

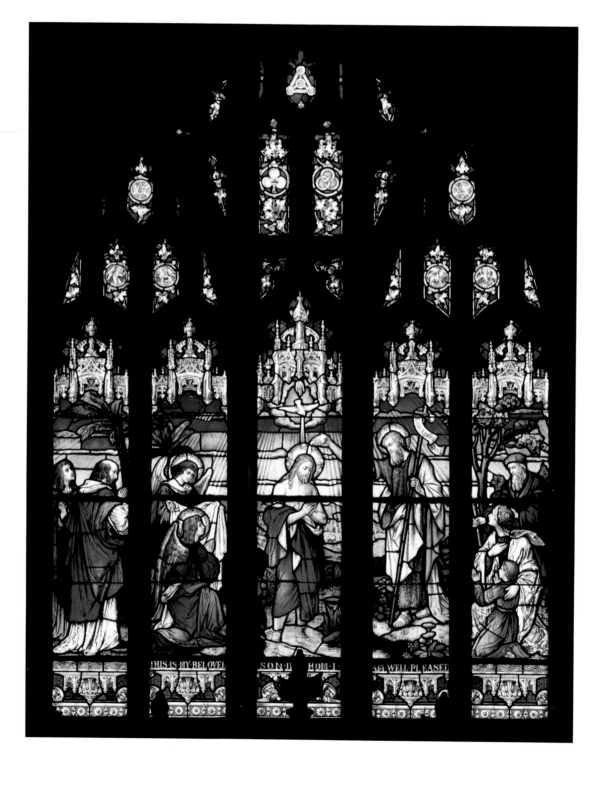

TRINITY EPISCOPAL

Address: 1519 Myrtle (Martin Luther King Boulevard) at Trumbull
Architect: Mason and Rice, 1892
Window: Baptism of Christ
Artist: Franz Mayer and Company, Munich, Germany, 1892

The most significant window in Trinity Episcopal, located at the east end above the altar, is illustrated here. It depicts the Baptism of Christ at the moment when the Three Persons of the Holy Trinity were present, a subject appropriate for a church dedicated to the Trinity. The large window is Gothic in style, its five lancets united by handsome tracery. The central lancet is devoted to the figure of Christ, above him a dove symbolizes the Holy Spirit, and above the dove is the hand of God: altogether representing the Holy Trinity. Jesus stands in the River Jordan while John the Baptist performs the Baptism. After the Baptism the heavens opened and Jesus saw the Spirit of God descending like a dove and heard a voice from heaven saying, "This is my beloved Son, in whom I am well pleased" (Mark 1:10–11). These words are written at the bottom of the three central lancets (partially obscured in the middle). This window is typical of the Munich School. The figures are monumental and realistic, the glass is a mixture of pot-metal and heavily painted glass, and the leading is not necessarily an integral part of the design. The Renaissance-style window is three dimensional, an effect aided by the landscape in the background. The canopies in all five lancets are architectural and done in silver stain. The openings in the tracery contain reminders of the Trinity. In the other lancets are angels and the crowd to whom John the Baptist was preaching. The colors are intense blues, purples, ruby, and gold.

A variety of other noteworthy windows grace the rest of the church. Among them are two windows in the south aisle, The Last Supper and An Angel and Mary at the Tomb, both signed by Willet Studios. The Apocalypse Window in the west wall, also designed and executed by the Willet Studios, is worthy of mention for its unusual history. Some twenty years elapsed between the design and the execution of this window. The cartoon, which had mysteriously disappeared, was found by a sexton rolled up behind a radiator in the church. It was returned to Willet Studios and the window was finally completed and installed in the 1960s. Another window of note is a lovely, sentimental window of Christ blessing little children, by

the Tiffany Studios, in the north aisle. The perspective in this window is created in part by the layering of glass and by the colors.

Ground for Trinity Church was broken in the spring of 1890 and the building was consecrated on New Year's Day 1893. The donor of the church was James E. Scripps, founder of *The Detroit News*. In the 1880s Scripps went to the southern counties of England with an architect to capture details and proportions of the fourteenth-century Gothic churches. Every part of Trinity is an artistic gem taken from some church of the English countryside. The church is constructed entirely of stone with a small amount of wood included. The sculptured heads at the door of the Trumbull Avenue porch entrance are of special significance. At the left is the head of King Richard II, a fourteenth-century English king, and at the right a portrait head of John Wycliffe, the first translator of the Bible into the English language. The exterior of the church also displays a series of grotesque gargoyles that serve as downspouts just as they did in medieval times. Each of them is different, some of them animal and some human. They represent fleeing evil spirits for it will be noted that they all point away from the church building. By contrast, inside the church ten carved angels supporting the wooden nave roof point inward toward the church. The interior has two side aisles and a clerestory supported by massive stone pillars. One pillar's capital has been left rough and unhewn as a perpetual reminder that the work of the Church is never done. The chancel ceiling is a barrel vault closely following that of the Chapter House at Canterbury Cathedral in England. The ceiling beneath the tower is vaulted with stone, probably the first genuine stone-groined vaulting in the United States.

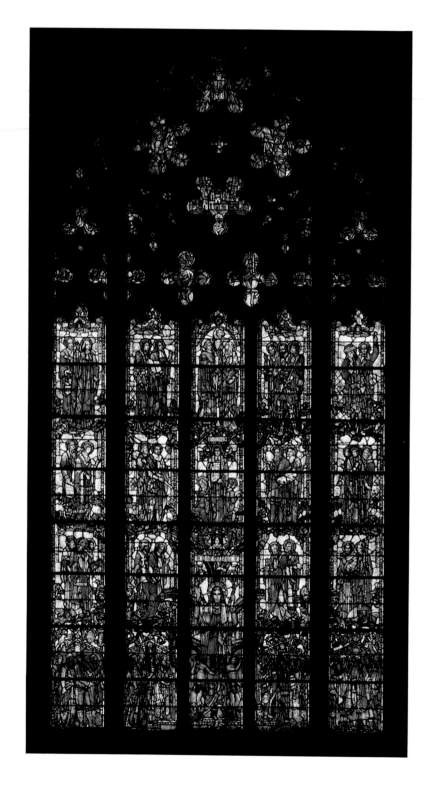

TRINITY LUTHERAN

Address: 1345 Gratiot at Rivard
Architects: W. E. N. Hunter, Don W. Hunter, and L. W. Simpson, 1931
Window: The Vine and the Branches, west window
Artist: Henry Lee Willet, Willet Studios, Philadelphia

The window above the choir gallery illustrated here, the Vine and the Branches, depicts Christ as the life of the Church. Christ, with the caption "I am the vine" above him, occupies the center panel of the window. At his feet on a smaller scale are Adam and Eve, the latter being tempted by Satan in the form of a serpent, while at the same time the serpent is being crushed beneath the feet of Christ. Below Christ and on either side of him is the procession of the nations with sixteen different nationalities represented; all the figures are looking up to the Son of God. The second row contains such figures as St. John, St. Paul, and Wycliffe; the third row depicts, among others, Martin Luther, John Hus, Lucas Cranach, J. S. Bach, and Thomas Cranmer; and the fourth row contains John Calvin, John Knox, and John Wesley plus more recent church workers such as Calvin F. W. Walther, Henry Muehlenberg, and Charles Krauth. The top of the center panel portrays symbolic parenthood. The tracery above the five panels of this large window includes scenes of Jerusalem and the Apocalyptic vision of Christ in Glory seated on his throne. Surrounding the figure of Christ are the twenty-four elders in sparkling raiment and the four horsemen of the Apocalypse—Death, Conquest, Famine, and War. The window is in rich multicolors, the pieces of pot-metal glass jewellike in size, and there is white glass included to allow enough light to enhance the play of the brilliantly colored glass.

The rest of the windows in the church are also Willet windows and continue the jewellike vibrant colors of the west window. The south clerestory contains Old Testament figures. Beginning from the altar in three-lancet windows are found John the Baptist, Isaiah, and Joel; Niehemiah, Daniel, and Jonah; Solomon, David, and Samuel; Job, Moses, and Abraham. In the north clerestory are found the New Testament figures. In three-lancet windows they are Peter, Paul, and John; Matthew, James, and Luke; Bartholomew, Thomas, and Phillip; Timothy, Eunice, and Barnabas; and Jude, Stephens, and Philemon. Over the altar in stained glass is a richly colored portrayal of the Resurrection and Ascension. Pictured in the small

aisle windows are emblems or reminders of Lutheranism and the life of the Christian. Delightful roundels of painted glass by the Detroit Stained Glass Works are found in the Community Room. They depict such arts as music, literature, wood carving, painting, architecture, and sculpture. The window of Norman slab glass in the pastor's study contains medallions showing age handing the torch of knowledge to youth. The window was made and donated by the Detroit Stained Glass Works.

Off the south aisle is a small lancet window known in Trinity Church as the Ruth Window. Charles Gauss funded the church building in thankfulness for the recovery of his fourteen-year-old daughter, Marion, from polio surgery. The window celebrates this event by depicting the story of Ruth with Marion as Ruth and her mother as Naomi. The window is signed by Henry Lee Willet.

The church is the third for the congregation of Trinity Evangelical Lutheran, the second one on this site. Designed in the style of a sixteenth-century English Gothic pier and clerestory with a triforium gallery, it is a perfect cathedral in miniature and one of the very few churches in Detroit to contain almost all the elements of a Gothic cathedral. If one plans on going to Europe to study cathedrals, a visit here is an excellent prelude. The building is constructed with variegated granite and limestone and some three hundred figures are portrayed on the exterior. Luther is shown in a stone figure on a turret along the Rivard Street exterior. The interior has a high narrow nave, flanked on either side by an aisle, and over which are the triforium and clerestory. The roof is of decorated wood, and suspended on chains from the hammerbeams are wrought iron and mica lamps. Also worthy of note are the church's fine carvings in both wood and stone.

TRUMBULL AVENUE PRESBYTERIAN

Address: 1435 Brainard at Trumbull
Architects: Hesse and Raseman, 1886
Window: Great North Window

The large four-lancet window on the church's north side (partially obscured by the balcony) is crowned by three large rose windows in the tracery. The rose windows are patterned in quatrefoil, that is, having four leaves or rounded corners. The numbers are symbolic, three being the divine number suggesting the Trinity, and four symbolizing the Four Evangelists. Except for the biblical scenes of St. Paul in prison in the center two lancets, the windows consist entirely of stylized floral and geometrical designs in vivid colors of reds, blues, greens, yellows, lavenders, and browns. The figure window to the left represents St. Paul raising his hand in blessing for the two who ask of him, "What must I do to be saved?" Paul answers, "Believe in the Lord, Jesus Christ, and thou shalt be saved." To the right, St. Paul in chains is writing one of the Epistles, his faithful friend Timothy at his side. The inscription reads, "For this cause, I, Paul, the prisoner of Jesus Christ for you Gentiles." The figures are large and realistic and the color of their robes intense purple, green, blue, and yellow. The far left lancet has a cross inscribed IHS, the first three letters of the name of Jesus in Greek. The lancet on the far right contains an elaborate crown, emblem of victory, with lilies rising from the center, symbol of the Ressurection. The church has two other large stained glass windows of similar floral and geometrical design and in the same brilliant colors. They also contain biblical scenes and emblems. The glass in all of these windows is pot metal and opalescent, the biblical scenes done in painted enamel.

Trumbull Avenue Presybterian Church is an offshoot of Fort Street Presbyterian Church. The present edifice was begun in 1886 and completed in 1888. The style is variously called Gothic and Byzantine. The exterior is of pressed brick with cut stone trim. The church interior had the largest auditorium of any Presbyterian church in the city at the time. After the addition of the gallery between 1889 and 1894, the seating capacity was 1,211. (The gallery, unfortunately, obstructs a complete view of the large stained glass windows.) The pews radiate outwardly in amphitheater style from the platform. The woodwork was originally all golden oak, and the stained glass windows, made in Chicago, were done in yellow tones to blend with the woodwork and the mustard yellow tone of the walls and ceiling. The hammerbeams, now painted over, and the Communion table wall are Carpenter Gothic in design. The pipe organ is located behind and above the Communion table. It is a Granville Wood instrument installed in September 1899 and made in Northville, Michigan. (This tracker-action organ is listed in the National Register of Historic Places.) A Sunday school building designed by the firm of Smith, Hinchman, and Grylls was added to the east end of the church in 1910.

On July 24, 1973, five stained glass windows were stolen from the church. Harold C. Vernon, the rector at that time, appealed in *The Detroit News* for their return. A woman in Birmingham responded to the appeal; she had purchased one of the windows from an antique shop in Detroit. A doctor at one of the hospitals in the Detroit area had two others. These three windows were returned and their purchase prices refunded. Two are still missing. One carried the name "Perkins" and is dated 1880. These windows are believed to have been purchased and taken to northern Michigan. They, too, contain patterns of floral and geometrical designs in colors of blues, yellows, greens, reds, and browns. It might be added that all church windows are vulnerable to thieves and vandals and it behooves all citizens to maintain a vigilant watch that stained glass windows remain in their rightful places.

III PUBLIC AND PRIVATE BUILDINGS

Following the Art Deco period of the thirties and the forties, American architecture rejected the decorative arts in favor of the "international style" of design. Imported from Europe and primarily of Bauhaus origin, this philosophy combined art and technology that virtually eliminated the artist-craftsman. The new style, coupled with severe changes in the economic structure of the country, meant that the woodcarver, the tile maker, the glass artist, and others found little use of their talents save some religious buildings whose limited budgets necessarily minimized their efforts. Handmade stained glass soon gave way to mass-produced colored glass, a factory product rather than an artistic one, and modern industrialized architecture advanced without the integration of the arts. The well-known precept that architecture is itself art of the highest order undoubtedly filled the gap.

Through the centuries, stained glass has been so intrinsically interwoven as a symbol of the worship environment that its application in other areas often places it out of context, again limiting its use. So it was perhaps inevitable that glass artisans and artists would disappear from the architectural scene in America. Very few artists and architects saw the immense value in stained glass as a superb medium to transmit light and color in abstract terms. Those who did were too small in number to prevent a virtual disappearance of stained glass as an element of architecture.

The seventies and eighties, however, brought two trends that could completely reverse events of the past fifty years with regard to stained glass and other art and architectural elements. One was an incredible resurgence in the concept of close collaboration and integration of art and architecture. A very powerful national movement to enrich our physical environment with art has given the arts industry in America a prominence never seen before. With ever-growing public support and awareness, it would seem inevitable that stained glass art will again find its place in architecture.

The second trend of this era is that which has been improperly described as the "post-modern era" in architecture. It generally constitutes a design regression to the twenties and the thirties when the decorative arts were so prominent. Today's architects are renewing the values of decoration that were excluded by the International Style. While architects have yet to fully rehabilitate the role of the artist-craftsman in their work, the craftsmen's greater involvement, if tended properly, is inevitable. Although painters and sculptors abound, it will be very interesting indeed to see if the artist-craftsman still exists to participate in this latest revival. The future is bright for those who will use it.

William Kessler
Fellow, American Institute of
Architects

GEORGE L. BEECHER HOUSE
(Now University Development Office, Wayne State University)

Address: 5475 Woodward
Architect: H. J. M. Grylls, 1893–1894
Window: Signed Tiffany Window, first floor landing of central staircase, ca. 1894.
Artist: Tiffany Glass and Decorating Company
(Photo courtesy of the Wayne State University Collections.)

The signed Tiffany stained glass window, designed by Frederick Wilson, in the Beecher House, is divided into three panels topped by three smaller panes and framed with dark oak. The large central panel is illustrated here. The subject is of a musical nature with a white-gowned allegorical figure embracing a cupid who is playing an instrument. Roses are strewn at the figure's feet. The background is a receding landscape with trees, hills, and sky. A pair of white doves flutter in the lower left foreground. The side panels contain torches, wreaths, and scrolls; motifs found throughout the house. The smaller panels depict lyres with a wreath flanked by elaborate scrolls. The dominant colors in the opalescent glass are blue, green, purple, and gold harmoniously blended, and are a bright contrast to the dark oak woodwork. In 1973 the window was cleaned and restored and Plexiglas panels were installed over the exterior surface, subduing the colors but protecting it from the elements.

The Beecher House was built by George L. Beecher, whose father, Luther, had amassed a large fortune in the dry goods business and at one time was reputed to be Michigan's largest taxpayer. Upon inheriting his father's fortune George Beecher purchased the Woodward property in 1893 and built his home there. The family occupied the house until 1914 after which it was converted into a boardinghouse. In 1947 it was purchased by the Children's Center of Metropolitan Detroit and in 1968 Wayne State University, the present owner, acquired it.

The Beecher House is a blend of classical and Italianate styles. The foundation of the building is coarse limestone rubble, typical of Italian Renaissance palaces, while the three-story superstructure is constructed of yellow brick and limestone topped by a pressed metal cornice with dentils, egg and dart, and modillions. The asymetrical facade consists of a flat-roofed tower at the south corner and limestone plastered bays. The interior decorating of the first floor makes extensive use of oak woodwork, wainscoting, and molded plaster. Every ceiling is of a different pattern of heavy molded plaster in elaborate floral designs with the exception of the library/dining room which has an oak-beamed ceiling. Torches, wreaths, and scrolls, reflected in the stained glass window, are decorative motifs used in the ceilings as well as other interior decoration. Dominating the airy grand hall is the open oak staircase where the Tiffany window shown here is located.

THE FRENCH LED by LA SALLE DISCOVER DETROIT

CITY OF DETROIT III'S *GOTHIC ROOM*

Location: Dismantled in 1956; reassembled and relocated in the Dossin
  Great Lakes Museum, Belle Isle
Naval architect: Frank E. Kirby, Detroit and Cleveland Navigation
  Company
Window: The La Salle Window
Artist: Frederick Keil, Edward F. Lee Glass Company, Detroit

In 1912, the *City of Detroit III* was the largest side-wheeler in the world. Forty percent of the ship's full width hung over the water enveloping the wheels. This gave extra space for staterooms, dining rooms, a grand salon, a forward salon, a palm court, a winery, and finally on the top deck, sandwiched between the stack casing, the Gothic Room, an ornate smoking room, containing the stained glass window illustrated here. The ship was dismantled in 1956 and its parts were sold. In 1965 a public subscription campaign acquired the Gothic Room pieces from Frank Schmidt of Cleveland who had bought large pieces of the ship's joinery work, including the forward Salon and the Gothic Room. The Gothic Room, including its famous La Salle Window, has been carefully and painstakingly restored to its original grandeur and installed in the Dossin Great Lakes Museum.

The La Salle Window is semicircular and encased in carved oak mullions and tracery. The center panel depicts La Salle on Detroit's shore accompanied by two priests, one of whom holds a Bible. The caption under him reads, "The French Led by La Salle Discover Detroit." Historical accuracy is perhaps stretched in this incident, for it is anyone's guess as to who was really the first white man to see the Detroit area. The best guess, however, is the young French explorer Louis Jolliet, who paddled down the lakes and through the Detroit River in the late summer of 1669. Jolliet on leaving the Detroit area met another party camped on the shore of Lake Ontario. The leader of this group was Robert Cavelier Sieur de la Salle. The two priests with La Salle separated from him and La Salle went on to the Ohio River. In 1678–1679 La Salle constructed a small armed merchant vessel, the *Griffon*, which he sailed through the Detroit River in August 1679, the first ship ever to traverse those waters. This is probably the incident captured here in stained glass, for the small boat, paddled by a seaman, has a carved griffin on its prow. The priest accompanying La Salle on this journey was Father Louis Hennepin, chaplain of the expedition, and it was he who named Lake St. Clair in honor of the Saint's birthday.

This five-panel window is typical nineteenth-century glass with large areas of painted and rolled glass in the Renaissance landscape painting style. La Salle is clothed in seventeenth-century cavalier dress, the two men behind him in priestly robes. In the two panels at the left, Indians with tomahawk, knife, and spear watch La Salle land on Detroit's lush shore of flowers and ferns. The two panels on the right depict two cavaliers on the river bank and a sailor paddling the griffin-prowed boat. The colors of the stained glass are strong blues, reds, greens, purples, and gold. A small panel added to the lower right hand corner reads: "La Salle window purchased for Museum by Louisa St. Clair Chapter DAR."

The *City of Detroit III* was designed by naval architect Frank E. Kirby, including the shape and location of all its public rooms. But the ship's sumptuous interiors were the work of the interior decorator, Louis O. Keil, the same Louis Keil who designed Christ Lutheran Church in Indian Village. Until he died in 1918 Keil finished all the big Kirby-designed side-wheelers on Lake Erie and the Hudson, as well as numerous smaller steamers. Keil's masterpiece was the *City of Detroit III*. Settings like the ornate Gothic Room regaled a passenger who had $3.50 for the fare from Detroit to Buffalo and a dollar more for an upper berth in one of the 430 staterooms.

CRANBROOK HOUSE

Address: 5510 Lone Pine Road, Bloomfield Hills
Architect: Albert Kahn, 1907
Window: Prodigal Son among Harlots, the Oak Room

George Gough Booth, publisher of *The Detroit News,* patron and donor of Christ Church Cranbrook, and creator of the educational complex of Cranbrook, asked Albert Kahn to design his home. Booth, also the first president of the Detroit Society for Arts and Crafts, encouraged fine craftsmanship and the production of beautiful objects, and the Cranbrook house incorporates several sixteenth- and seventeenth-century Flemish stained glass panels. The small panel, illustrated here, is a sixteenth-century panel, circular in shape, representing a feast scene and depicting an episode from the story of the prodigal son. Of all the parables this one is the most often reproduced in art, teaching the virtues of repentance and forgiveness. This continuously popular theme is first found in the stained glass of the thirteenth-century cathedrals of France. The subject matter of the Prodigal Son among Harlots is common in Netherlandish painting of the sixteenth and seventeenth centuries. This exquisitely detailed small panel of the son feasting with harlots at an inn and losing the last of his inheritance, is stained in light tones of yellow, orange, and brown, and enclosed in a border of Renaissance designs, with figures of putti (cupid figures) among floral scrolls. Do note the amorous couple in the background. The panel is 13.5 inches in diameter and comes from the Delannoy Collection of Belgium. It was purchased by Booth in 1939 and is located in the room known as the Oak Room because of its "linenfold" paneling (featuring a texture resembling flatly folded cloth) carved by John Kirchmayer of Cambridge, Massachusetts, who also carved the panels in the family library. Among the other art objects in the Oak Room is the blue and white Chinese plate on the mantel which the family used for over seventy years to serve plum pudding at their Christmas parties. For the past twenty years it has been used for the same purpose at the Twelfth Night celebrations for all Cranbrook Educational Community staff members, faculty, and other employees.

Cranbrook House was planned as a family home for George G. and Ellen Scripps Booth and their five children. In 1908 the Booths moved into Cranbrook House, so called after the village of Cranbrook in Kent, England, whence George's grandfather had emigrated in 1844, and they became the first year-round residents of Bloomfield Hills, then a farm and summer residence community. The solidly built house, originally consisting of what is now the central portion with the west and south wings added later, was furnished in the heavy, ornate style of its time. Formal, dark English furniture, much of it upholstered in fine tapestries or needlepoint designs, was used throughout with the influence of the Arts and Crafts Movement felt in each room. All the furnishings in the rooms are the original ones. Albert Kahn's design for the home evolved from plans to which the whole Booth family had contributed suggestions and ideas, particularly with regard to the English manor style.

Booth, whose formal schooling ended at the age of fourteen, recognized the value of education, and together with his wife Ellen Scripps Booth, daughter of the prosperous newspaper publisher, James E. Scripps, worked to create the unique educational and cultural complex known today as the Cranbrook Educational Community.

DETROIT PUBLIC LIBRARY

Address: 5201 Woodward
Architect: Cass Gilbert, 1921
Window: North Wall of the Adam Strohm Hall
Artist: Frederic J. Wiley, 1925

The painted-glass windows in the Adam Strohm Hall are one of the most beautiful features of the Library's interior decoration. Originally nine windows graced the hall, although today only six are visible. In the Detroit Public Library's pamphlet *Library Service* (vol. 8, no. 5, May 1, 1925), Frederick J. Wiley, the designer, gives the following explanation of the significance of their ornamental detail:

> It was the custom of printers of Renaissance times to preface their books with an initial page containing the title of the book surrounded with a design of formal or fanciful ornament illustrative of the book's content. This practice has been kept in mind in designing this series of windows. In some places ornamental details used in the windows have been copied from book covers, illuminated manuscripts and printers' devices. The nine windows form three groups of three windows each, each containing a central somewhat more elaborate window with a simpler window on each side of it. Poetry, Art, Music, Science are noted in different places and the continuity of the series is suggested by the signs of the zodiac which start at the south side and continue in sequence around the room. The designs of the windows are similar, but the details have considerable variety; their similarity conforms to the character of the room, and the variation in the ornament hints at the diversity of subjects which make up the contents of the books continually passing in and out of the library.

Of the three windows in the north wall, the central one, illustrated here, bears the Latin inscription "Quo ducit lux" (meaning "Whither does the light lead"). It is designated "Art" and has characters representing musical notes. The central decoration is set in a sculptural frame resting on griffin-like creatures at the base and topped by birds that resemble storks. This frame suggests exquisite wrought iron grilles. An archangel at the top of the window frames the word "Art." The left window has a quotation from Milton's "Il Penseroso" at the top: "And Cynthia checks her dragon yoke." The central figure here is Thalia, muse of comedy. The inscription above reads "Cynthia." The upper part of the right window quotes from Shelley's "Hymn to Apollo": "I walk upon the mountains and the waves." The central figure is Erato, the muse of love poetry, and the inscription above is "Apollo."

Of the three windows in the south wall, the central window has above the figures the Latin word "Aspiro," meaning "I aspire." The central figure is Melpomene, the muse of tragedy, and the central figure in the window to the right is Euterpe, the muse of lyric poetry.

The most pretentious and ornate of the windows once filled the west wall immediately above a finely chiseled bronze grille and clock. Since 1965 these three windows have been obliterated by an immense mural by John S. Coppin titled "Man's Mobility." It is a very interesting mural but large in detail and detracts from the six delicately wrought windows of the north and south walls. The mural on the east wall by Gari Melchers, done in 1921, is delicate in both color and detail and complements rather than detracts from the six remaining windows.

All of the windows are "quarry windows," which means that they are made of painted glass cut into squares after the Italian Renaissance manner and are in harmony with the architecture of the rest of the building. The general color scheme of the windows is a light gray, with touches of bright colors. They achieve their original purpose, the admission of white light into the room.

In 1915 a competition for the design of the Detroit Public Library was won by Cass Gilbert, a leading architect in the American Renaissance revival style. Inspired by Gilbert's student days in Italy, the Detroit Public Library is a synthesis of the works of the architectural giants of the Italian Renaissance. Its white Vermont marble facade is a model of carefully studied proportion and detail. The original building, begun in 1917, was completed in 1921. The Cass Avenue addition, a simpler version of the classical revival style, was the work of Cass Gilbert, Jr., Francis Keally, and the W. B. Ford Associates and was completed in 1965.

EDSEL & ELEANOR FORD HOUSE

Address: 1100 Lakeshore Road, Grosse Pointe Shores
Architect: Albert Kahn, 1926–1929
Windows: Heraldic shields and heraldic panels, stairwell

This English heraldic stained glass is fifteenth-century glass, rare in Detroit and especially rare in a private home. The architect has brilliantly displayed the stained glass within a setting reminiscent of quarry windows. Quarry windows were an extension of grisaille windows and great favorites of fifteenth-century England. The quarries were diamond shaped, and individually decorated with small stained glass emblems which might include flowers, insects, leaves, and heraldic devices. The Ford windows are a leaded-diamond pattern in clear glass with the wealth of heraldic blazons in various colors and designs placed in them to capture the best possible effect in the extraordinarily beautiful setting of the Ford House. The four upper windows in the Ford House stairwell contain the heraldic devices illustrated here. The first panel, the medallion on the far left, has a yellow saltire, a St. Andrew's cross, that divides the shield into four compartments. The second panel is shieldlike in design and is divided into four segments. The first and fourth segments each contain lions rampant in azure on a yellow background. The second and third contain three white pike fish in each. The third heraldic panel, also shieldlike, contains a single large yellow lion rampant on an azure background. The entire shield is cut diagonally by a bar of red and white glass. Seven fleur-de-lis surround the lion. The fourth panel is medallion shaped with a shield in the center. A white chevron divides a ruby background containing ten silver crosses. (Nicholas Rogers, a heraldry consultant from Cambridge, England, has identified all the shields in the Edsel & Eleanor Ford House. His technical descriptions of the stairwell windows, observing the well-established rules of the exact science of heraldry, appear in the glossary.)

The gallery in the house contains one panel of fourteenth-century date (unique in Detroit) and twenty-one pieces of English heraldic glass of the sixteenth century. All are expertly situated in diamond-patterned leaded clear glass windows. The cloister contains a delicate medallion in silver stain, dated 1542, depicting the Madonna and Child.

When the Fords decided to build their lakeshore home, they had two basic ideas. They wanted a modest and picturesque home—not a palace or fortress—and they wanted to reproduce faithfully the beautiful and practical Cotswold houses of Worcestershire, England. The result was one of the very rare and sophisticated revivals of the era. In 1976 Eleanor Clay Ford donated her home to be used for the benefit of the public and established a trust for its maintenance. The Edsel & Eleanor Ford House, as it is known now, is one of the finest of the homes built by the automobile industry magnates and the only one still standing in the Grosse Pointe area. The collection of buildings comprising the estate was designed by Albert Kahn of Detroit who began his career designing factories for the automobile companies. In addition to his industrial work he designed a number of public buildings in Detroit and Ann Arbor which still stand and are considered models of fine revival architecture. His best-known Detroit works are the Fisher Building and the General Motors Building in the New Center Area.

The Ford House contains many elements taken from period houses in England, such as antique paneling, fireplaces, architraves, chimney breasts, and staircases. The house is faced with Briar Hill sandstone. The roof is of stones imported from England. Expert workmen were also imported to split the stones and lay them in authentic Cotswold manner. With the exception of the antique paneling the house was completed in 1927. The intricate fitting and installing of these interior walls consumed nearly another two years and the family did not move into the house until 1929. In addition to the workmanship, the home preserves for posterity fine examples of paneling from the sixteenth, seventeenth, and eighteenth centuries and the Modern Room is an outstanding work of Art Deco by a leading designer of the twentieth century, Walter Dorwin Teague. Except for some extraordinarily valuable paintings that Eleanor Ford gave to the Detroit Institute of Arts, the house remains as it was decorated by the Fords, and it still contains paintings by Cézanne, Matisse, Raphael, Franz Hals, and Redon. The grounds of the House were designed by Jens Jensen, a leading landscape architect of the time and a proponent of naturalistic plantings with native plant materials and no exotics. His work always contained a stately and elegant meadow lined with elms.

GUARDIAN BUILDING

Address: 500 Griswold
Architect: Smith, Hinchman, and Grylls, 1929
Window: The Fidelity Window, elevator lobby

The Union Trust Building, now the Guardian Building, completed in 1929, once was known as the Cathedral of Finance. In keeping with its cathedral image it has two large stained glass windows in the north-side elevator lobbies. These windows, almost identical in design, were recently rediscovered when the Michigan Consolidated Gas Company, in its careful restoration of the building, removed dropped ceilings placed there by a former tenant, bringing to light two windows that had been totally obscured. A monumental stylized figure dominates each window, one symbolizing security (to serve as a guard) and the other fidelity (to reassure the public of loyalty, constancy, and truth). In keeping with the Aztec motif of the building the figures are clothed in American Indian feathered cloaks with arms upraised, and each holds a diamond-shaped shield on which is inscribed either "Security" or "Fidelity." The windows are of rolled glass in intense blue, green, and gold colors with painting limited to the face, hands, and feet. As surrounding buildings now partially obscure the light, newly designed artificial lighting aids in a dramatic presentation of these windows.

The Guardian Building, a thirty-six-story structure, was Detroit's great Art Deco experiment and still is one of the best examples of Art Deco architecture in the country. The first widely popular style to break with revivalist tradition, Art Deco is essentially noted for its decoration. In Europe the forms were inspired by Cubism; in the United States the inspiration was North and South American Indian art. Its influence upon Wirt Rowland was obvious as he developed the decorative scheme for the building. He helped formulate the red-tan "Guardian Brick" used in the main portion of the building. At the sidewalk level is a two-foot sill of Somes Sound granite from Maine. Above this is a six-foot band of Montrose granite from Wisconsin, then another band of Somes Sound, above which is Mankato stone from Minnesota to the sixth story. An ornamental band of green, tan and red-brown terra-cotta and glazed tile was placed above the Mankato stone. These tiles are used throughout the building. Rowland worked closely with Mary Chase Stratton of Detroit's Pewabic Pottery Company in formulating the different tiles used throughout the building.

Stepped arches crown the building's entrances. The central design in the main entrance is a conventionalized figure symbolizing progress and in the smaller medallions are portrayed the three divisions of commercial activity—industry, agriculture, and transportation. Over the Congress entrance the tile contains a beehive symbolizing thrift and industry, an eagle (taken from a gold coin of the United States) representing money, and a caduceus (alluding to the staff of Mercury, messenger to the Gods), a symbol of authority.

The building's interior is dramatic. The walls of the main lobby start with a band of Belgian black marble at their base. Numidian marble caps this band and Mankato stone tops the marble. The rare Numidian marble was chosen for its unusual blood-red color. No working mine quarried the marble, and in order to obtain it Rowland went to Africa and reopened a mine that had been closed for thirty years. The mosaic mural in the main lobby was designed by Ezra Winter, who also designed the great mural in the main banking room. The vaulted ceiling of the lobby is made of Rookwood tile from Cincinnati and matches the Pewabic exterior tiles. Two flights up from the entrance lobby is the main banking room. The mural for the 150-foot vaulted ceiling was designed by Detroiter Thomas DiLorenzo and painted by Anthony Eugenio, an Italian immigrant. The original lighting fixtures are amber glass from Czechoslovakia. The giant columns in the room were formed from travertine marble imported from Italy, and the black marble forming their base was from Belgium. At one end of the banking room stands an ornamental grille of Monel metal that holds at its center a large clock backed with Tiffany favrile glass. The same glass appears in the elevator doors.

In 1975 Michigan Consolidated Gas Company purchased the Guardian Building and determined to restore it to its original 1929 splendor. Alfred Glancy III, Consolidated's chief executive officer, predicts that by the end of the 1980s "things will be as they should be with a building of this calibre." 137

FRANK J. HECKER HOUSE
(Now Smiley Brothers Music Company)
Address: 5510 Woodward at East Ferry
Architects: Scott, Kamper, and Scott, 1890
Window: Floral stained glass window on the landing of the grand staircase

A grand staircase rises from the colonaded reception room of the Frank J. Hecker House to a landing dominated by this large stained glass window. This handsome window is simply crafted in a floral and arabesque design in yellow stained glass of various hues, from pale gold to almost brown, on a palely tinted opalescent glass background. It is composed of a large rectangle flanked by two narrow rectangles on either side with a horizontal rectangle and two small squares at the top. In the four corners of the large center rectangle are delicate arrangements of flowers in various hues of yellow and in the middle is a stylistically designed wreath, below which is a small winged face. Most of the central window, however, is composed of pastel opalescent glass that glows with the colors of milky opals but that also allows ample light for the grand staircase. The flanking rectangular windows are filled with arabesque and floral decorative designs in various hues of yellow very much in the fashion of Tiffany's decorative windows. The leading is fine and graceful as befits the delicately designed pattern of the window. The yellow tones against the opalescent background is a very effective contrast to the rich brown wood of the grand staircase. The window is a lovely Victorian touch in an elegant French Renaissance chateau.

Colonel Frank J. Hecker, a handsome and distinguished veteran of the Civil War and the Spanish American War, came to Detroit along with his friend Charles Lang Freer in 1879 with little capital and large ideas for starting a company to build railroad freight cars. With Hecker as president and Freer as vice president their company, the Peninsular Car Company, prospered and both men retired in 1899 millionaires many times over. The two friends built architecturally noteworthy houses next door to each other on Ferry. The Hecker House now belongs to the Smiley Brothers Music Company and the Freer House is part of Wayne State University.

Hecker's wealth was assured by 1888 when he enlisted Detroit architect Arthur Scott to design a home for him befitting one of the city's leading industrialists. Scott sought the help of Louis Kamper of McKim, Mead, and White of New York. Kamper, recognizing Detroit's French heritage, recommended the architecture of the French renaissance for inspiration and suggested the Hecker home be modeled on the general outlines of the Chateau de Chenonceau sur le Cher—Cher, a tributary of the Loire. Chenonceau was the home of Diane de Poitiers, adored mistress of King Henry II of France.

In 1890 the glistening white limestone towers and steep gray roofs of Hecker's new mansion rose on the edge of the city. The beautifully carved detailing struck a new note of sophistication in Detroit's Age of Elegance. The Hecker home of three stories and a basement consists of forty-nine rooms, covering more than 54,678 square feet. The hall paneled in white oak, the oval dining room in mahogany, the library in English oak with matching graining, the parlor and music room finished in white and gold, the fireplaces of Egyptian Nubian marble and onyx, and the vestibule wainscoted in Italian Siena marble exist today almost identically to the way they were finished by architect Louis Kamper in 1890. (Kamper also designed the Book Cadillac Hotel, the Book Building, the Book Tower, the Washington Boulevard Building, the David Broderick Tower, and many private residences in Detroit.)

Hecker died in 1927 at the age of eighty-one, and in 1947 the Smiley brothers took over the Hecker property. They are credited with restoring the estate with meticulous and loving care. A major renovation undertaken by the Smiley brothers is the carriage house, which is now a two hundred-seat concert hall, including three practice rooms for the use of music students and teachers in the community.

McADOW HOUSE
(Now the church house of the First Unitarian-Universalist Church)

Address: 4605 Cass at West Forest
Architect: John Scott, 1892–1893
Windows: Two-story Bay Windows

The McAdow House is an example of the solid, constrained, but opulent dwellings popular with Detroit's affluent citizens at the turn of the century. The broad Elizabethan-style staircase rises from the hall in a short flight of steps to a spacious landing lit by the two-story stained glass windows illustrated here. The staircase boasts eight windows in all, the four at the bottom are rectangular, the four immediately above are rectangular with rounded heads. They are reminiscent of Tiffany's style with the sinuous designs of the Art Nouveau period. The lower four windows are lightly tinted glass with delicate graceful leading. The lower part of the upper windows continue in a similar motif, but higher up the windows display stylized floral patterns in arabesque. The glass is both pot metal and opalescent in shades of pastel yellows, blues, and lavenders, and thus sufficient light enters the great square hall that served as the McAdow's living room. The windows may have been influenced by the Tiffany windows at Cass Avenue Methodist Church built one year earlier a short distance away.

Another notable example of stained glass in the McAdow House is a lunette (a semi-circular panel) of a young woman's face found above a hallway door. Designed by a Detroit artist named Garnsey, it was executed by the Taylor Studios of New York and is entitled *Unshed Tears*. It is thought to be a portrait of someone who died in the McAdow House.

Other interesting decorative features of the first floor of the house are the painted lunette panels over each door that sometimes depict scenes appropriate to the function of the room: cupids over the entrance, books and scrolls above the library door, classical vases and flowers indicating the drawing room, fruits representing the dining room, a hunting scene over the door to the service wing, and a palette and brush above the door to the former elevator. The stained glass windows in the hall and the painted lunettes over the hall doors are representative of the Arts and Crafts Movement of the late nineteenth century when much attention was given to detail and handcrafted work.

The McAdow House was built by Mr. and Mrs. Perry W. McAdow in 1892. It is a two-and-a-half-story, hip-roof, red-brick and brownstone, rectangular building of Renaissance Revival design by architect John Scott, who also designed the

Wayne County Building. The interior of the house is elaborately decorated in the English Renaissance style with massive carved-wooden fireplace breasts, an open Elizabethan-inspired staircase with beaded openwork railing, and beamed ceilings. The floor plan is in the Queen Anne style with large formal rooms opening from the spacious living hall. The second floor contains three large bedrooms, and the half-story third floor holds a billiard room and a ballroom. In all, the house contains twenty-two rooms and twenty-three closets.

The McAdows were an interesting couple. A Detroiter, Clara McAdow was a doctor's widow, living in Billings, Montana, when in 1884 she met and married Perry McAdow, a merchant who owned a small share in a Montana gold mine. A shrewd and ambitious woman, the new Mrs. McAdow managed the couple's modest beginnings, and she was instrumental in accumulating their great wealth and ultimately in acquiring ownership of the entire gold mine. In 1892, temporarily leaving her husband in Billings, Clara McAdow returned to Detroit, purchased the half block from Prentis to Forest on Cass, and began the construction of her new home. Like many other nouveau riche of the period the McAdows built this house as a means for entering Detroit Society. Unfortunately, Clara never attained her goal, for she died in 1896. In 1897 the house was sold to Mr. and Mrs. Frederick Stoepel who, in turn, sold it to Mr. and Mrs. Horatio Hovey in 1904. The Hoveys occupied the property until 1913 when they sold it to the Universalists Congregation which used the house as a temporary church until a new edifice could be erected in the garden to the north. Since the new church was completed in 1916 the McAdow house has served as the church house. It is now listed on both the National and Michigan Registers of Historic Places. The entire property, three buildings and the grounds, is a City of Detroit Historic District.

STROH BREWERY COMPANY

Address: Buildings demolished, 1986
Architect: Attributed to Spier, Rohns, and Gehrke, 1912
Window: Heraldic Window, now in Stroh Brewery Company
*   Headquarters, 100 River Place*
(Photo courtesy of Stroh Brewery Company.)

The stained glass window illustrated here was designed and executed by the Detroit Stained Glass Works for the Brew House of Stroh's Brewery. It was installed in 1914. The same company made a copy in 1956 to be placed at the opposite end of the Brew House. The center panel contains a lion rampant holding a sword in silver stain on a shield of ruby glass. Above are a crown, orb, and cross. The name "Stroh Brewery" appears on a background of creamy opalescent glass above the cross. The center panel is surrounded by a decorative floral border in Art Nouveau style, containing hops, barley, and vines. This is in green and gold opalescent glass.

The emblem of the lion rampant dates back to the early days of the brewery when it was known as the "Lion Brewery." The lion crest came from Kyrburg Castle in Kirn, Germany, the town from which Bernard Stroh, Sr., emigrated, moving first to Brazil and then to Detroit in 1850. When the company name changed to Stroh Brewery Company in 1902, the lion was kept as the company emblem.

Bernhard Stroh, Sr., came to Detroit by chance. His chosen destination was Chicago, but a port call by the lake boat on which he was traveling convinced him to settle in Detroit. He began brewing in a small way at 57 Catherine Street in the German section of the city. His family had been brewers in Kirn, Germany, since at least 1775, so, like many of his compatriots, he arrived in America with a skill. At first, Stroh brewed his lager beer in a copper kettle that held slightly more than a full barrel. The beer, in small kegs, was delivered by wheelbarrow around the neighborhood. At that time there was no known method of preserving the product for an extended period, so the brew had to be sold locally.

Stroh prospered, and by 1865 he purchased land on Gratiot Avenue near his small brewery. The Lion Brewery was established there in 1870. A new Brew House and stock houses were built in 1912 and located on the same spot. It was there that the "fire brewed" beer was made. There were only two companies that made beer by this method in 1974, Stroh and the Urquell Brewery in Pilsen, Czechoslovakia. The Brew House had nineteen copper brew kettles, each with a 250-barrel capacity, set in Pewabic tile. With the closing of the plant in May 1985, brewing in Detroit ceased. The company headquarters at 100 River Place and the ice cream operation remain in the city. It is interesting to note that at the turn of the century Detroit was the home of twenty-three breweries. Now there are none.

Stroh survived the Prohibition by changing its name to Stroh Products Company and producing near beer, malt extract, soft drinks, ice, and ice cream. When the sale of beer was legalized in 1933, Stroh's changed its name back to Stroh Brewery Company and resumed the brewing of beer. All the other operations then ceased except for the production of ice cream.

DAVID WHITNEY, JR., HOUSE

Address: 4421 Woodward at West Canfield
Architect: Gordon W. Lloyd, 1890–1894
Window: Tiffany windows in the first-landing stairwell
Artist: Tiffany Glass and Decorating Company

The three windows illustrated here depict the figure of an "explorer" in the central window flanked by decorative windows of scrolls and arabesques. The dashing explorer, dressed in seventeenth-century French costume could be Antoine de la Mothe, Sieur de Cadillac, who entered the Detroit River on 23 July 1701. The figure is clothed in bright, rich colors of opalescent glass and framed with yellow scrolls and arabesques. The windows on either side are opalescent and pot-metal glass in yellows and browns. These decorated windows afford sufficient light to enhance the dark rich colors of the bearded explorer.

All the stained glass windows in the Whitney House are from the Tiffany Studio. Tiffany was a favorite decorator of the rich, and it was, therefore, predictable that when lumber baron David Whitney, Jr., decided to build an "American palace" in the Romanesque revival style he would also choose Tiffany to design the windows, despite the fact that Tiffany's Renaissance realism and the opaqueness of his opalescent glass were hardly appropriate for a Romanesque building.

Some of the most attractive windows are in the music room. Represented there in the four stained glass windows of opalescent glass are St. Cecelia, patroness of music; cherubs and a harp; Apollo with his lyre; and cherubs and a zither. A small heraldic window depicts pipes, trumpets, and laurel leaves. All four windows in the second stairwell are decorated in scrolls and arabesques in the same manner as the two that frame the explorer, discussed above. The dining room contains heraldic panels placed in clear glass. In the drawing room, the large windows of clear glass are topped by smaller windows in delicately colored and gracefully leaded stained glass.

The Whitney House was a dream which took four years to create, and Whitney was to enjoy it for only six years before he died. It is a massive three-storied structure built of jasper stone, a variety of pink granite from South Dakota. It features a multigabled and turreted roof, arched and decorated windows on the upper story, and porches with polished jasper columns. Jasper stone, all hand cut, is so hard that a small blacksmith shop was maintained during construction for continuous sharpening of tools. The interior of the house is made up of forty-two rooms, containing twenty marble and onyx fireplaces, stained and leaded Tiffany glass windows, carved wood decorations, parquet floors, and a grand staircase with a bronze balustrade. The most impressive room, the Grand Hall, has a massive mantlepiece with an inset bronze clock. Originally the interior walls were decorated with silks, tapestries, and other art objects. The second floor consists of a ballroom and several bedrooms. The third floor was once an art gallery displaying Whitney's large collection.

Behind the main house stands the Carriage House, the largest such edifice in the state. After the Whitney family ceased living in the home in the 1920s the house served as headquarters for the Wayne County Medical Society, which sold it to the Visiting Nurses Association in 1957. Kughn Enterprises bought the house in the late seventies and restored it as nearly as possible to its original opulence. The mansion now houses a three-storied restaurant in the grand manner of cruise ships like the *S.S. France.*

IV STAINED GLASS STUDIOS

All artwork balances between creative endeavor and commerce. On one end of the scale are the weekend painter and the artist-recluse who never shows his work. On the other end are highly competitive companies, operating with large overheads, including huge invoices for painter's canvas by the roll, foundry services, or tons of lead caming and thousands of square feet of colored glass.

The stained glass studio weighs heavily toward the commercial side of the scale: ancient Guild tradition, labor-intensive production, monumental scale, and costly materials. Can art thrive—or even survive—in such a climate? Yes it can, and it has. Economic worries notwithstanding, there is a lot about the studio situation that actually helps beautiful work happen: giant drawing-walls for full-size "cartoons"; large stocks of glass that permit great freedom and sensitivity in the choice of color; and plenty of extra hands to keep the work moving smoothly toward completion. Unfortunately, there are also plenty of instances where studio business concerns have obstructed or even negated both the artist's vision and the needs of the client. Studio owners with one eye on the clock and the other on the inventory have filled many a church with uninspired, and uninspiring, work.

Because time and economics are so much intertwined in the creation of stained glass, it takes a deep commitment to esthetic and spiritual values to outweigh the elements of commerce. How far should the studio go in attempting to express the work's full measure of originality and vitality? Studios that were founded or controlled by artists of merit have not been afraid to answer "as far as necessary." This attitude did not mean that they were unsuccessful in business. Tiffany Studios, for instance, ran at top speed for over twenty years until the changing styles and falling fortunes of the 1930s closed them down. Connick Studios in Boston and Willet's in Philadelphia continued to do excellent work long after their artist-founders passed on. They accomplished this by upholding their original high standards, and by knowing how much to charge for the extra time, effort, and expense that fine work requires.

The ancient stained glass in the great cathedrals of Europe has impressed and inspired worshipers for centuries. New work for modern worship spaces can do the same for genera-

Mark S. Talaba

tions to come, but only if there are both studios and clients willing to commit their resources to the right side of the scale.

Mark S. Talaba
Stained glass artist
Mark Talaba Studios

CHARLES J. CONNICK ASSOCIATES, DESIGNER AND WORKERS IN STAINED, LEADED, AND FACETED GLASS, 1913–1986

Charles Jay Connick was born in Springboro, Pennsylvania, in 1875 and died in Boston in 1945. From childhood he had demonstrated a great interest in drawing and, when obliged to leave high school in Pittsburgh, he became an apprentice artist on the *Pittsburgh Press*. At the time the old chalk plate system of engraving was in vogue and this rough approximation of an etching was genuine training in the use of expressive line, a technique that was to serve Connick well when he turned to producing stained glass windows in 1894, as an apprenticeship in the shop of Rudy Brothers in Pittsburgh.

Orin Skinner, who succeeded Connick as president of Connick Associates, is quoted as saying that, although Connick never finished high school, he "was one of the best educated men I ever met. He knew and loved the classics, had a passion for good poetry, and a deep appreciation of music." Connick studied life drawing and painting in night classes and went to Europe to study stained glass, ancient and modern, in the cathedrals of England and France. On his return he made windows from his own designs in various shops until 1913, when he opened his own studio in Boston, where he worked during the remainder of his life. Connick did much to raise the standard of stained glass craft in the United States and was a pioneer in the renaissance of medieval glass. He rejected the use of opalescent (opaque) glass, then the rage, favoring antique glass in which color is transparent and which provides, through brilliant light, a vibrating pattern of vivid beauty. The tendency of his work in glass was modern but it was related in spirit to the masterpieces of the twelfth and thirteenth centuries. Some of the artist's most successful windows were those he produced for St. Patrick's Cathedral and St. Vincent Ferrer in New York City. His greatest work is considered to be the west rose window, forty feet in diameter, for the Cathedral of St. John the Divine, also in New York. Connick adopted Pegasus, the mythical winged horse, as his symbol. He designed it in stained glass and it was carved on his gravestone after he died in 1945. Following his death his studio became a cooperative with each craftsman becoming a part owner. Orin E. Skinner became president, a post he retained until Charles J. Connick Associates, Designer and Workers in Stained, Leaded, and Faceted Glass, closed its doors in 1986. The studio's records can now be found in the Boston Public Library, and Connick's writings and lectures are summarized in his book *Adventures in Light and Color* (1937), an introduction, history, and appraisal of ancient and modern glass.

Examples of Connick windows in Detroit are in the Cathedral Church of St. Paul, Metropolitan Methodist Church, Holy Redeemer Church, All Saint's Episcopal Church, Saint Mary of Redford Church, Woodlawn Mausoleum, and the Young Women's Christian Association (YWCA) Chapel.

THE DETROIT STAINED GLASS WORKS, 1861–1970

The Detroit Stained Glass Works was established in 1861 by Charles Fredericks and Peter Staffin, under the name of Friedricks and Staffin. In 1878 "Detroit Stained Glass" became part of the firm name. Friedericks was born in Germany in 1838 and came to the United States in 1844; Staffin was born in Erie County, New York, in 1841. Together they engaged as glass stainers for churches, dwellings, steamboats, and railroad cars, as well as producing decorative stained glass products of all other kinds. They advertised that "customers may furnish original designs, which will be produced in stained glass without extra charge, and such designs will not be duplicated by the firm for other orders." In 1896 Staffin left the company and moved to Ann Arbor and Edward Wolfram joined the firm which then became Friedericks and Wolfram. In 1909 they incorporated as the Detroit Window and Stained Glass Company. Wolfram left the firm in 1914, and the firm became known as the Detroit Stained Glass Works, the name it retained until it closed its door in 1970. During its history the Detroit Stained Glass Works did business in Michigan, Ohio, Indiana, Kansas, Alabama, California, and Colorado. They also had a factory in Windsor, Canada. Records of the Detroit Stained Glass Works can be found in the Burton Historical Collection in the Detroit Public Library.

Examples of stained glass designed and executed by the company can be seen in such Detroit churches as Sweetest Heart of Mary, St. Joseph's, St. Francis of Assisi, Sacred Heart, Holy Redeemer, St. Cecelia, Old St. Mary's, Trinity Lutheran, St. John's, and St. Paul's in Grosse Pointe, and also in the heraldic window of the Stroh Brewery Company headquarters.

Joseph Lamb

THE J. AND R. LAMB STUDIOS, 1857—

P. O. Box 291
Philmont, New York 12565

The J. and R. Lamb Studios, founded in 1857 by Joseph and Richard Lamb, sons of an English landscapist, is now the oldest continuously operating stained glass studio in the United States. When Karl Barre Lamb, Joseph's grandson, died in 1969, it appeared that it would be necessary to close the business just as other contemporary studios such as Tiffany and Connick had been forced to do. As an alternative Lamb Studios offered itself for sale to its employees, and that's how Donald

Samick, the present owner, acquired the firm in 1970. Katherine Lamb Tait, whose grandfather was one of the founders of the studio, and who was active there as a stained glass artist and designer until her death in 1981, once said that she felt a strong continuity as though the studio were still being run by the Lamb family. (Tait designed the east window in Mariners' Church, Detroit.)

Architect Donald Samick's first association with Lamb Studios was as an interior designer of religious structures, and this association inspired his deep appreciation of the role of stained glass in church architecture. One of the most cherished traditions of the Lamb Studios, which Samick continues to foster, is the artistic quality of its work. The artists represent a wide variety of styles and all are able to perform any of the operations involved in producing stained glass. In the course of a week, an individual craftsman may cut patterns, work at the glass bench, paint glass, fire it, or solder and glaze. No one is confined to a single activity but may, like the artist, stay with a project through all its phases. This is not only more interesting for the craftsman, but also makes for better craftsmanship and pride in work done. Lamb Studios can design and produce an interior space, including woodwork and ornamentation, and create the stained glass which can be either according to a client's own specifications or custom designed by the Lamb artists. The techniques range from Renaissance to ultramodern. The client list of the Lamb Studios is as international as its work force, and since the studio's inception it has produced more than ten thousand windows for buildings in each of the United States and in twelve foreign countries.

Lamb Studios has executed stained glass windows for some thirty churches in the Detroit area, including Mariners' Church, St. Andrews Memorial Episcopal Church, Fort Street Presbyterian, St. John's Episcopal, Cathedral Church of St. Paul, St. Joan of Arc in St. Clair Shores, and Beth Abraham Synagogue in West Bloomfield.

FRANZ MAYER AND COMPANY, 1848—

25 Seidl Street
Munich, West Germany

In 1848 Joseph Gabriel Mayer founded the Establishment for Architecture, Sculpture, and Painting under the probable patronage of King Ludwig I of Bavaria. Royal commissions for the Cologne and Regensburg cathedrals and the Maris Helf Kirche in Au soon prompted J. G. Mayer, his son Franz Borgias, and his son-in-law F. X. Zettler, to expand the establishment by including a division for stained glass. In 1882 King Ludwig II conferred on the firm the title of "Royal Bavarian Court Institution." Under the direction of Franz Borgias Mayer the firm (now known as Franz Mayer and Company) attained its highest international fame for art glass. Still in the family today, the company is now headed by Gabriel Mayer, a direct descendent of the founder, and continues to design and execute windows in all styles and techniques—medieval, contemporary, and also naturalistic.

The thousands of stained glass windows executed by Franz Mayer and Company for cathedrals, churches, and chapels all over the world include: by order of Pope Pius X in 1912, a stained glass window for St. Peter's Church in Rome, Italy, representing the dove, symbol of the Holy Ghost, surrounded by golden rays; a number of windows in four chapels of the North American College in Vatican City; and many of the stained glass windows in Roman Catholic cathedrals in cities of the United States, such as Buffalo, Cleveland, Covington, Los Angeles, San Francisco, St. Augustine, and Spokane. Mayer windows in churches and chapels are represented in the Detroit area at Duns Scotus Seminary, St. Boniface Roman Catholic, St. Florian, St. Cecelia, Our Lady of Lourdes Church, Cathedral Church of St. Paul, Church of the Messiah, Christ Church–Detroit, and Trinity Episcopal.

TIFFANY GLASS AND DECORATING COMPANY, 1892–1930

Louis Comfort Tiffany (1848–1933), son of Charles Lewis Tiffany, the New York jeweler, studied art in Europe as well as with George Innes, the American landscapist, at the National Academy of Design in New York. He remained a dedicated painter all his life and his landscape paintings metamorphosed into glass later in his career. Tiffany began his career as an avantgarde decorator in 1881, introducing the Art Nouveau style to his wealthy patrons and in the public rooms of the White House. His interiors often included glass mosaics, stained glass windows, and lighting fixtures. This predilection for glass ultimately led to the formation of the Tiffany Glass and Decorating Company in 1892, and Tiffany produced his first Favrile glass

152

in 1896. (Favrile, a Tiffany trademark, means "handmade.")

The creation of opalescent glass in the 1870s was independently arrived at by both Tiffany and John La Farge (1835–1910), and enabled the artists to make glass containing exaggerated textures and color variations, and then to use those variations as part of their compositions. La Farge probably deserves the credit for first conceiving the idea of window designs based on patterning and variations within the glass itself. However, opalescent windows based on abstract and geometrical designs were introduced by Tiffany, who is also considered the creator of the landscape windows in opalescent glass. Tiffany experimented extensively, developing every kind of glass he could imagine. Some glass was wrinkled and folded before it cooled so as to look like drapery, some was rippled to suggest water, and other efforts resulted in sky glass and sunset glass. Some combinations he developed even suggested marble. Eventually the Tiffany Company had thousands of sheets of different kinds and colors of glass, all about three feet long, all color coded and stored so that the right glass could be found to suggest any effect Tiffany wanted. He used the brush only for detail and shading.

Tiffany glass reached the zenith of its popularity between 1900 and 1921. After that time popular tastes turned to the Bauhaus School of functionalism and to neo-Georgian architecture, and there was no longer a demand for stained glass and, in particular, for Tiffany products. During the Great Depression the Tiffany Company filed for bankruptcy. Tastes change, however, and a landmark sale in 1966 at Parke Bernet Galleries in New York reestablished Tiffany as an artistic force on the national and international art market, and it remains so to this day.

Tiffany stained glass windows in Detroit are found in the following churches: Cass Community United Methodist, St. Matthew & St. Joseph's Episcopal Church, St. John's Episcopal, First Presbyterian, and Christ Church–Detroit. Other buildings with Tiffany glass include the Whitney and Beecher houses, and the Wayne County Building.

THE WILLET STAINED GLASS STUDIOS 1898—
10 East Moreland
Philadelphia, Pennsylvania 19118

William Willet (1867–1921) founded the Willet Studios in Pittsburgh in 1898 and moved it to Philadelphia in 1912 where

William Willet

it remains to this day. Willet, together with his wife Ann Lee Willet, did great pioneer work in the revival of traditional craftsmanship and the renewal of interest in medieval glass. He first designed in opalescent glass but became convinced that while offering a fascinating and even beautiful effect, opalescent glass did not lend itself to genuine window design because its lack of translucency violated the primary reason for a window's existence—the admission of light.

Upon William Willet's death in 1921, his son Henry Lee Willet (1899–1983) left college to assume his father's place. He served as president until 1965, working with his wife Muriel Crosby Willet, his son E. Crosby Willet, and his daughter Ann Willet Kellog. Internationally known in his field, Henry Lee Willet was a restless missionary, lecturing and traveling and arranging exhibitions to further the cause of medieval glass. Under his direction Willet Studios, a one-family enterprise since its incorporation in 1898, expanded from the original complement of a dozen artist-craftsmen to become the largest stained glass studio in the United States. Since 1965 E. Crosby Willet, son of Henry Lee, has been president of the company, now an independent unit of the Hauser Company of Winona, Minnesota.

The Willet Studios have continuously experimented in modern glass, utilizing many new methods, including dalle-de-verre, a bold and scintillating technique calling for simple shapes and strong colors in designs that are often abstract or semiabstract. The studios' own invention of "sculptured gold" windows combines stained glass with metallic sculpture or repousse (literally beaten up from the underside). The fact that the sculptured lead surface has been covered with twenty-three karat gold leaf is the secret of the windows' brilliant night effect. The process realized Henry Lee Willet's dream to design a unique window that would be beautiful by day or night. There are two examples of this type of window in the Detroit area, one in Westminster Presbyterian Church, Detroit, and the other in Memorial Church, Grosse Pointe Farms.

Detroit has many examples of windows by the Willet Studio. The very early windows of William Willet are found in the Church of the Assumption, Jefferson Avenue Presbyterian Church, Most Blessed Sacrament Cathedral, and Metropolitan Methodist Church. Among the more than fifty churches and other buildings in the Detroit area with windows executed under Henry Lee Willet's direction are Trinity Lutheran, Central United Methodist, Christ Church–Detroit, St. Catherine and St. Edward, St. Cecelia, St. Matthew's and St. Joseph's Episcopal, Trinity Episcopal, Christ Church Grosse Pointe, First United Methodist Church, Harper Memorial Hospital, and Woodlawn Mausoleum.

153

OTHER STAINED GLASS STUDIOS
Contributors of Windows to Churches and Buildings in Detroit

Bavaria Art Glass Studios, Minneapolis: St. Anne Roman Catholic

Buffalo Stained Glass Works, Buffalo: St. Anne Roman Catholic

Burnham Studios, Boston: Kirk in the Hills, St. Mary's of Redford; Sacred Heart Chapel (Grosse Pointe); Christ Church Cranbrook

D'Ancenzo Studios, Philadelphia: St. Cecelia; Christ Church Cranbrook; First Presbyterian

Daprato Studios, Chicago and New York: St. Charles Borromeo

G.T.A., Innsbruck, Austria: St. Anthony Catholic Church

Gorham Studios, New York: St. John's Episcopal

Ludwig von Gerichten, Columbus, Ohio: Holy Cross

Heaton, Butler & Bayne Studios, London, England: Cathedral Church of St. Paul; Christ Church Grosse Pointe

Hinicki & Smith, New York: Temple Beth El

Kase Company, Philadelphia: St. Florian

Frederick Keil, Edward F. Lee Glass Company, Detroit: *City of Detroit III*'s Gothic Room

La Farge Studios, New York: Church in the City

Gabriel Loire Studios, Chartres, France: St. John's Armenian; Our Shepherd Lutheran

A. Maglia Studios, Detroit: St. Matthew's & St. Joseph's Episcopal Church; Holy Family Roman Catholic

Munich Studios, Chicago: St. Paul's Catholic (Grosse Pointe)

Ranieri Studios, Detroit: Christ Church Grosse Pointe

Joseph G. Reynolds and Wilbur Herbert Burnham, Boston: Kirk in the Hills

Conrad Schmidt Studios, Milwaukee: Nativity of Our Lord Church

Mark Talaba Studios, Birmingham, Michigan: St. Scholastica Chapel, Evergreen Lutheran Church

Thompson Glass Company, Detroit: St. Albertus

Whitefriars, London, England: St. Peter Episcopal Church

Frederic J. Wiley: Detroit Public Library

J. Wippell & Company, Exeter, England: St. John's Episcopal, Christ Church-Detroit

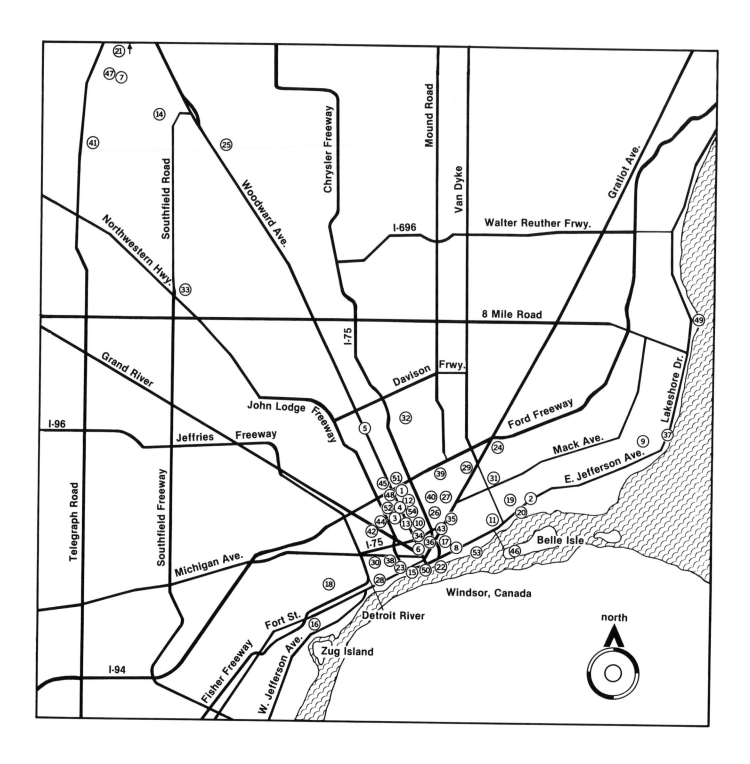

Glossary

AISLE A part of a church parallel to the nave and divided from it by piers or columns.

AMBULATORY Semicircular or polygonal aisle running around the eastern end of a church behind the altar.

ANNEALING Final cooling process in glass manufacture.

ANTIQUE GLASS Handmade, blown glass that has the irregular, crumbly texture of medieval glass.

APSE Semicircular or polygongal eastern end of a church.

ARPENT A United States standard of measure equal to 192.24 feet.

ART DECO A style identified with the 1920s and 1930s. It includes an exotically decorative side as well as streamlined, machine-inspired geometry. In Europe the forms were inspired by cubism, in the United States by North and South American Indian Art.

ART NOUVEAU Name given to a distinct decorative style popular at the end of the nineteenth century. Introduced in the United States by Louis Comfort Tiffany, the new style was applied to everything from inkwells to buildings. It is characterized by floral forms and fluid, waving, asymmetrical lines.

BAPTISTRY A part of a church; formerly a separate building used for baptism.

BAROQUE STYLE Architectural style of seventeenth and early-eighteenth centuries, characterized by curves and extravagant ornamentation.

BASILICA Originally a large, oblong Roman assembly hall, often with a semicircular apse; in Early Christian and later architecture a church built on this plan.

BAUHAUS A German art school reorganized after World War I by architect Walter Gropius. He renamed it the Bauhaus, meaning architecture house, and turned it into a technical school of design.

BEMA In churches and synagogues a raised platform for the clergy. In later church architecture it was developed to form embryonic transepts.

BLAZON In heraldry a coat of arms or armorial bearing.

BOTTLE GLASS *See* Norman slab.

CAMES (CALMES) Strips of lead used in stained glass windows.

CAMEO GLASS Two-layered glass; when carved the upper white layer stands in relief against the darker background.

CAMPANILE A bell tower that is detached from the body of the church.

CANOPY Glass framework within a window imitating an architectural niche and surrounding figures or a scene.

CARTOON Full-size design for a stained glass window.

CATHEDRAL GLASS Commercial, machine-rolled stained glass widely used in the United States.

CHANCEL Part of a church reserved for clergy and containing the altar.

CHRIST'S PASSION The last events of Christ's earthly life, from his entry into Jerusalem to his burial, are collectively called The Passion.

CHOIR The part of a church in which choris-   159

	ters sit, usually separated from the nave by a screen or rail; sometimes applied to the whole chancel.
CINQUEFOIL	*See* Foil.
CLASSICAL REVIVAL	Pertaining to the art and architecture of ancient Greece and Rome.
CLERESTORY	The upper part of the nave, transepts, and choir of a church containing windows; also any similar windowed wall or construction used for light and ventilation.
COFFERED CEILING	A design of indented panels usually in a flat ceiling.
CROCKET	In Gothic architecture, carved projections in the shape of stylized leaves that decorate the edges of spires, gables, and pinnacles.
CROWN GLASS (SPUN GLASS)	Blown glass, rare today, spun into a flat disc with a thick central knob.
CUTLINE	Tracing of the lead-line pattern from the cartoon.
CYLINDER GLASS	*See* Muff glass.
DALLE-DE-VERRE	Pieces of glass, usually about one inch thick and often chipped or faceted on the surface, which are set into epoxy, epoxy resin, or concrete.
DENTILS	A series of rectangular, projecting blocks that form a molding.
DIAPER WORK	An overall surface decoration composed of a small repeated pattern such as lozenges or squares.
EGG AND DART	A continuous banded design of alternate, engaged ovoids and arrowheads carved in high relief.
ENAMELING	Application of enamel paint to glass.
FAVRILE GLASS	Iridescent glass, patented by Tiffany in the 1880s, produced by the exposure of hot glass to metallic fumes and oxides.
FENESTRATION	The arrangement of windows in a wall.
FIRING	Process of heating painted glass so that the paint and the glass fuse smoothly and securely.
FLASHED GLASS	Two-layered glass, the bottom layer of white or light-colored glass and the thinner top layer of a darker color.
FOIL	Small arc opening in Gothic tracery; the number of the foils is indicated by a prefix–trefoil (3), quatrefoil (4) cinquefoil (5).
FOLIATED	Decoration with leaf ornamentation or a design comprising arcs or lobes.
FOUR EVANGELISTS AND THEIR SYMBOLS	Matthew (Man); Mark (Lion); Luke (Ox); and John (Eagle).
FUSED GLASS	Pieces of colored glass bonded to a sheet of glass by heat.
GARGOYLE	In Gothic architecture, a projecting stone waterspout, often in the form of a grotesquely shaped head of man or animal.
GEORGIAN	The style reflecting Renaissance ideals. It was made popular in England by the architect Sir Christopher Wren and began in the United States with the construction of the Wren Building at the College of William and Mary in 1695. The style became the Federal style after the Revolutionary War.
GOTHIC REVIVAL	Style of architecture, dating from the mid-twelfth century, generally associated with the pointed arch, the flying buttress, and the rib vault; it revived in the later half of the nineteenth century.
GRISAILLE	Clear glass ornamented in muted colors with delicate, often foliar patterns that is leaded into decorative designs. The word is derived from the French "grisailler," meaning to paint gray.
HALATION	Phenomenon in which light-colored glass surrounded by darkness or solid masonry produces a blurred effect, the light seeming to spread beyond the actual boundaries of the glass.
HERALDIC DESCRIPTIONS	The heraldic panels in the windows of the Edsel & Eleanor Ford House stairwell are described here in accord-

ance with the well-established rules of the exact science of heraldry. "Stairwell window 1: Azure a saltire or (Abbey of St. Albans). Stairwell window 2: Or a lion rampant azure (Percy, Earl of Northumberland) and gules three lucies hauriant argent (Lucy) quarterly. Henry Percy, 2nd Earl of Northumberland, or one of his descendants. The Lucy quartering was introduced as a result of his grandfather's 2nd marriage to Maud Lucy. Stairwell window 3: Azure flory and a lion rampant or over all a bend company argent and gules. Either Sir Henry Beaumont, Lord Beaumont (d. 1339/40), his son John, Lord Beaumont (d. 1342), or the latter's son Henry, Lord Beaumont (d. 1369). The 4th Baron Beaumont and his successors bore these arms without the bend. Stairwell window 4: Gules a chevron between ten crosses paty argent (Berkeley)." (This information was contained in a report by Nicholas Rogers to the Corpus Vitrearum Committee of the National Gallery, Washington, D.C., October, 1986.)

INTERNATIONAL STYLE — A style based on modern structural principles and materials. Concrete, glass, and steel are the most commonly used materials.

ITALIANATE HOUSE — At its most elaborate, the Italianate house had a low roof, overhanging eaves with decorative brackets, an entrance tower, arcaded porches and balustraded balconies. At its simplest, it was a square house with a low pyramidal roof, bracketed eaves, and perhaps a lantern or cupola.

JESSE TREE — Genealogical tree, showing Christ's descent from Jesse, popular in many forms of medieval art including stained glass.

LANCET — Tall, slim, pointed window.

LEADED GLASS — Small panes of glass held in place with lead strips (cames); the glass may be clear or stained.

LIGHT — Opening between the mullions of a window.

MANDORLA — An upright almond shape found chiefly in medieval art to enclose a figure of Christ enthroned.

MEDALLION WINDOWS — Windows composed of variously shaped small panels, often arranged in narrative sequence.

MODILLION — An ornamental bracket or console used in a series to support the upper member of a Corinthian cornice.

MUFF GLASS (CYLINDER GLASS) — Most commonly used form of stained glass; produced by cutting off the end of an elongated balloon of glass which is then split along its length to form a flattened sheet.

MULLION — A vertical stone shaft separating, and often supporting, lights.

NARTHEX — Western arcaded porch or vestibule in basilican churches.

NAVE — The long narrow main part or central aisle of a church, extending from entrance to transept or choir.

NORMAN SLAB (BOTTLE GLASS) — Glass blown into a square mold, each side of which is cut into a sheet of glass. It is rarely used today.

OCCHIO — A small round or, more usually, oval window; also known as Italian eye window.

OPALESCENT GLASS — Glass, developed in the late-nineteenth century by John La Farge and Louis Comfort Tiffany, in which streaks of color, when fused, give a milky, iridescent appearance.

ORDER — Any of several specific styles of classical and Renaissance architecture characterized by the type of column used (for example, Doric, Ionic, and Corinthian).

PEWABIC TILE — Tiles with iridescent glazes created by Mary Chase Stratton at her studio,

	Pewabic Pottery, on East Jefferson Avenue. Founded in 1903, the studio is still in existence.
PILASTER	A shallow pier attached to a wall; often decorated to resemble a classical column.
POT GLASS, OR POT METAL	Antique glass colored throughout with one color.
PREDELLA	A secondary painting or picture forming the border of a principal one. The lower part of a window usually containing a symbol or subject complete in itself.
QUARRY WINDOWS	Windows made of painted glass cut into square or diamond-shaped panes; used particularly in grisaille windows.
QUATREFOIL	*See* Foil.
REPOUSSE	In metalwork a technique for decorating a surface by hammering the reverse side of the object.
REREDOS	An ornamental screen behind the altar.
ROCOCO	Eighteenth-century development of baroque architecture, characterized by proliferation of ornamental details.
ROMANESQUE REVIVAL	Architectural style based on the techniques of Roman architecture and characterized by round arches and thick columns and walls.
ROSE WINDOW	Circular window with tracery radiating in petallike shapes.
ROUNDEL	Circular panel of glass.
SANCTUARY	Applies to the part of the church about the altar or communion table. It is also called the chancel.
SCAGLIOLA	Plasterwork in imitation of ornamental marble, consisting of ground gypsum and glue that is colored with marble or granite dust.
SILVER STAIN	Silver compound, usually silver nitrate, which when fused to glass produces a yellow color.
SPUN GLASS	*See* Crown glass.
STIPPLING	Method of painting that creates the effect of minute points of light all over the glass.
TRACERY	Ornamental stonework in the upper part of a Gothic window.
TRANSEPT	Two projecting arms, usually between the nave and chancel of a cruciform church.
TREFOIL	*See* Foil.
TRIFORIUM	Arcaded gallery below the clerestory, sometimes glazed, facing on to the nave.
TRIPTYCH	A set of three paintings or bas reliefs, related in subject matter, connected side by side, and usually designed as a movable altarpiece.
WHEEL WINDOW	Round window in which stone tracery radiates from the center like the spokes of a wheel.

Bibliography

Andrews, Wayne. *American Gothic*. New York: Random House, 1975.
———. *Architecture in Michigan*. Detroit: Wayne State University Press, 1982.

"An Exhibition of the Work of the Late Wright Goodhue." *Stained Glass* 27, no. 3 (1932): 91.

Armitage, E. Liddall. *Stained Glass: History, Technology, and Practice*. Foreword by Richard Coombs. Newton Centre, Mass.: Charles T. Branford, 1959.

Baker, John. *English Stained Glass of the Medieval Period*. London: Thames & Hudson, 1978.

"Beauty in Stained Glass." *Michigan Living* (April 1982):9–11.

Charles Connick Associates. Records. Boston Public Library, Boston, Massachusetts.

Clark, Robert Judson. *The Arts and Crafts Movement in America, 1876–1916* (catalogue). Princeton, N.J.: Princeton University Press, 1972.

Connick, Charles, *Adventures in Light and Color: An Introduction to the Stained Glass Craft*. Foreword by Charles D. Maginnis. New York: Random House, 1937.

Cortissoz, Royal. *John La Farge: A Memoir and A Study*. New York: Houghton Mifflin, 1911.

Cowen, Painton. *Rose Windows*. San Francisco: Chronicle Books, 1979.

Cram, Ralph Adams, *My Life in Architecture*. Boston: Little, Brown, 1936.

Detroit Stained Glass Works. Papers. Burton Historical Collection, Detroit Public Library, Detroit, Michigan.

Farmer, Silas. *History of Detroit and Wayne County and Early Michigan: A Chronological Cyclopedia of the Past and Present*. Detroit: Gale Research Company, 1969.

Ferguson, George. *Signs and Symbols in Christian Art*. New York: Oxford University Press, 1966.

Ferry, W. Hawkins. *The Buildings of Detroit*. Detroit: Wayne State University Press, 1968.

Hanks, David A. *The Decorative Designs of Frank Lloyd Wright*. New York: E. P. Dutton, 1979.

"Historical Churches in Detroit," *Michigan Living* (December 1981):14–16.

Lamb, Frederick S. "The Making of a Modern Stained Glass Window—Its History and Process." *Craftsman* 10 (April 1906): 18–31.

Lamb Studios. Archives. Philmont, New York.

Lee, Lawrence. *The Appreciation of Stained Glass*. London: Oxford University Press, 1977.

Lee, Lawrence et al. *Stained Glass*. New York: Crown Publishers, 1976.

Lloyd, John Gilbert. *Stained Glass in America*. Jenkintown, Pa: Foundation Books, 1963.

Lynes, Russell. *The Art-Makers of Nineteenth-Century America*. New York: Atheneum Publishers, 1970.

McKean, Hugh. *The Treasures of Tiffany*. Chicago: Chicago Review Press, 1982.

Metropolitan Museum of Art Bulletin. December 1971/January 1972.

Meyer, Katherine Mattingly, ed. *Detroit Architecture: A.I.A. Guide*. Rev. ed. Detroit: Wayne State University Press, 1980.

Scheyer, Ernest. *The Circle of Henry Adams: Arts and Artist*. Detroit: Wayne State University Press, 1970.

Skinner, Orin E. "Connick in Retrospect." *Stained Glass* 70, no. 1 (Spring 1975): 16–19.

Sturm, James L. *Stained Glass from Medieval Times to the Present: Treasures to Be Seen in New York*. New York: E.P. Dutton, 1982.

Weinberg, Helene. "John La Farge and the Invention of American Opalescent Windows." *Stained Glass* 67, no. 3 (1972): 4–11.

Willet, Henry Lee. "Henry Lee Willet, Troublesome Fellow." *Stained Glass* 73, no. 1 (1978): 23–26.

Willet Studios. Archives. Philadelphia, Pennsylvania.

Woodford, Frank B. and Woodford, Arthur M. *All Our Yesterdays*. Detroit: Wayne State University Press, 1969.

Index